Giovanni Sartori

ECPR Press

ECPR Press is an imprint of the European Consortium for Political Research in partnership with Rowman & Littlefield International. It publishes original research from leading political scientists and the best among early career researchers in the discipline. Its scope extends to all fields of political science, international relations and political thought, without restriction in either approach or regional focus. It is also open to interdisciplinary work with a predominant political dimension.

ECPR Press Editors

Editors

Ian O'Flynn is Senior Lecturer in Political Theory at Newcastle University, UK.

Laura Sudulich is Senior Lecturer in Politics and International Relations at the University of Kent, UK. She is also affiliated to Cevipol (Centre d'Étude de la vie Politique) at the Université libre de Bruxelles, Belgium.

Associate Editors

Andrew Glencross is Senior Lecturer in the Department of Politics and International Relations at Aston University, UK.

Liam Weeks is Lecturer in the Department of Government and Politics, University College Cork, Ireland, and Honorary Senior Research Fellow, Department of Politics and International Relations, Macquarie University, Australia.

Giovanni Sartori

Challenging Political Science

Edited by Michal Kubát and Martin Mejstřík

London • New York

Published by Rowman & Littlefield International, Ltd.
6 Tinworth Street, London SE11 5AL
www.rowmaninternational.com

In partnership with the European Consortium for Political Research, Harbour House, 6-8 Hythe Quay, Colchester, CO2 8JF, United Kingdom

Rowman & Littlefield International, Ltd. is an affiliate of
Rowman & Littlefield
4501 Forbes Boulevard, Suite 200, Lanham, Maryland 20706, USA
With additional offices in Boulder, New York, Toronto (Canada), and London (UK)
www.rowman.com

Selection and editorial matter © Michal Kubát and Martin Mejstřík, 2019
Copyright in individual chapters is held by the respective chapter authors.

All rights reserved. No part of this book may be reproduced in any form or by any electronic or mechanical means, including information storage and retrieval systems, without written permission from the publisher, except by a reviewer who may quote passages in a review.

British Library Cataloguing in Publication Information
A catalogue record for this book is available from the British Library

ISBN: HB 978-1-78552-287-1
ISBN: PB 978-1-78552-286-4

Library of Congress Cataloging-in-Publication Data Available

ISBN: 978-1-78552-287-1 (cloth)
ISBN: 978-1-78552-286-4 (pbk.)
ISBN: 978-1-78552-288-8 (electronic)

Contents

Preface   vii
    Giovanni Capoccia

Introduction   1
    Michal Kubát and Martin Mejstřík

1. Giovanni Sartori: A Giant of Political Science   13
    Gianfranco Pasquino

2. An Italian in New York, an Alien to Political Science?: An Intellectual Portrait of Giovanni Sartori   27
    Michal Kubát

3. The Applicability of Political Science: Sartori's Insight   41
    Martin Mejstřík

4. Giovanni Sartori and the Democracy of the Italian Second Republic   53
    Oreste Massari

5. Giovanni Sartori and Party Theory   69
    Klaus von Beyme

6. Sartori's Typology of Party Systems and Its Challenging Legacy: The Model of Polarised Pluralism and the 'Invisible' Politics   81
    Maxmilián Strmiska

7. Is the Consensus Model of Democracy Better for All Countries?: On Sartori's Critique of Lijphart   91
    Miroslav Novák

8	Giovanni Sartori as a Political Theorist: On His Polemics with Marxism *Marek Bankowicz*	105

Conclusion 117
Michal Kubát and Martin Mejstřík

References 121

Index 131

About the Contributors 139

Preface

Giovanni Capoccia

This collection brings together a series of essays on the life and work of Giovanni Sartori, written by scholars from several different generations for whom his work has served as a source of inspiration. Unlike most *Festschriften*, it accompanies the celebration of the honoree's work with broader reflections on the tensions existing between Sartori's intellectual legacy and the current state and direction of political science. In general, many political scientists would agree that the depth and the originality of Sartori's work have not found the recognition in the discipline—in particular in the United States—that their rigour and originality would have warranted. Most contributions to this volume deepen and articulate this narrative while repositioning it as a 'challenge' to modern political science, implicitly warning that today's political scientists forget Sartori's lessons at their peril.

The pessimistic view of Sartori's influence on contemporary political science should probably not be exaggerated: many of Sartori's writings have been translated into several languages and are still among the most cited in the discipline. A quick search on Google Scholar shows that ten of his works have citations in the thousands, and more than a further forty in the hundreds. In the United States, David Collier's work at Berkeley, developing Sartori's framework for conceptual analysis, should be mentioned as one important example of how his legacy continues to be valued. Other examples of how Sartori's work has been recognised across the Atlantic, where he taught for nearly two decades, are also worth a brief mention. In 2006, the 'Qualitative and Multi-Methods Research' Organized Section of the American Political Science Association organised a very well-attended roundtable on Sartori's intellectual legacy, on which I participated together with David Collier, John Gerring, Gary Goertz and Markus Kurtz. On that occasion, the Section bestowed Sartori with its Lifetime Award, for which he expressed delight and gratitude in his acceptance speech. Collier and Gerring's 2009 edited volume *Concepts and Methods in Social Science: The Tradition of Giovanni Sartori* reprinted his main methodological works and complemented them with essays of younger-generation comparativists who have applied and extended his work.

Be all that as it may, it is true that, all things considered, the state of political science today does not reflect Sartori's vision for the discipline and that the forefront of the discipline bears limited traces of his theoretical and methodological preoccupations. In his long and prolific career, Sartori certainly did not shy away from disciplinary polemics: everybody who knows his work will be acquainted with his criticisms of what he saw as unproductive directions of analysis becoming predominant in the discipline and the neologisms ('degreeism', 'novitism', 'cat-dog' are among the most memorable ones) produced by his *vis polemica* in the course of the debates that engaged him over the decades. And in spite of the above-mentioned recognition of his work, as well as other acknowledgements, which attest to his continued influence among comparativists, it is not unlikely that Sartori would use similarly colourful adjectives to describe today's general state of the discipline.

Yet the context of the rough-and-tumble of disciplinary polemics and oft-changing academic fads may not be the best one for assessing Sartori's overall intellectual contribution. Even though he may have lost several professional battles, many of Sartori's works—on conceptual analysis, democracy, party systems and other themes—continue to be read and to serve as a source of inspiration several decades after their publication. Very few authors in the social sciences are able to stand the test of time. This privilege is reserved for those publications that are rightly honoured with the epithet of 'classics' of a discipline, a category to which Sartori unequivocally belongs. And even fewer authors inspire books of comments—or even criticism—like this one, which is not the first, and will most likely not be the last, to engage with Sartori's legacy.

Of course, it is not a prerequisite to be inadequately recognised during one's lifetime (a characterisation that is at any rate only partially true in Sartori's case) to later earn the status of a 'classic'. The history of any discipline, in the social sciences and beyond, and indeed of any intellectual field, contains examples of classic authors who were on both the winning and the losing side of the professional battles that they fought during their lifetime. In Sartori's case, however, it is probably fair to say that exactly some of the reasons that likely contributed to making his work less fashionable in the short run may be among the main causes for the durability of his intellectual work in the long run: its rootedness in long-standing traditions of philosophical and logical thought; its tackling of big, important questions that are relevant for politics and not just for academic debates; its capacity often to transcend disciplinary boundaries and narrow methodological debates to appeal to a broader audience, academic and otherwise. For these reasons, Sartori's work is likely to remain, for future generations, a source of inspiration, criticism, even imitation. Although his work will not appeal to all political scientists—indeed, it is hard to imagine any figure able to do so in the theoretically and methodologically fragmented field of political science—it will certainly endure for many comparativists, as well as for many others beyond the boundaries of our discipline.

Introduction

Michal Kubát and Martin Mejstřík

This volume pays tribute to one of the founding fathers of contemporary political science, Giovanni Sartori (1924–2017). Sartori was a member of a shrinking generation of prominent figures in the field, a generation that included the late Robert Alan Dahl, Maurice Duverger, Samuel Phillips Huntington, Juan José Linz and Seymour Martin Lipset. In manifold ways, Sartori helped lay the theoretical and conceptual foundations of political science and the social sciences in general.

In pop culture, we often read about 'legends', be they in films, rock bands or other undertakings. In most cases, this is a marketing gimmick, as one 'legend' replaces another in a heartbeat. We have all experienced the temporality of something being 'legendary'. Indeed, to come back to the point, there are only few truly legendary film stars or rock bands. Giovanni Sartori was such a rare legend. Already during his prolific life, Sartori became an icon of political science and was recognised as such by both his peers and his students. In the past, extensive homages (Passigli 2015; Pasquino 2005) were published in his honour, and Sartori received a number of prestigious awards and high-ranking distinctions (for example, the Prince of Asturias Award in 2005 and the Karl Deutsch Award in 2009). Many scholars have examined his work (Amato et al. 1991; Collier and Gerring 2009a; Pasquino 2014), and Sartori himself has become the subject of analysis (Pasquino 2009; 2013a). This volume is both a continuation and an extension of the analysis of the lifework of Giovanni Sartori, focusing on the imprint the recently deceased 'giant' has left on political science.

A careful reader will notice the rather diverse topics covered by the individual chapters of this book, reflecting Sartori's equally diverse interests in public affairs. To be sure, Sartori's interests were broad, when it comes both to theoretical issues and to the everyday practice of politics. Sartori was not a scholar confined to teaching and writing for other academics. He was a prolific journalist and essayist, an organiser of scholarly and university life, and a stubborn and fearless warrior for political science as a discipline. In this volume, we argue that what he was as a person influenced his work, which as a result is thematically broad and multilayered. In his scholarship, Sartori addressed not only comparative politics and political theory but also the methodology of the social sciences. That being said, how to fit all of it into one volume? Indeed, given the scope of Sartori's scholarship, every work about him and his work will need to be selective. This volume's selections are based on what made Sartori 'Sartori', and as such it includes some chapters that dwell on his theoretical writings and others that present him more broadly as an engaged intellectual. While no compilation can do justice to the richness of Sartori's life and work, this volume provides scholars of political science with a rich overview of his struggles, achievements and legacy. Given the quantitative direction of contemporary political science, it aims to open a window to new scholarly debate on the discipline.

But really, what is it that made Sartori into the embodiment of political science, a provocative thinker and a relentless activist? What turned Sartori into 'Sartori'? What this volume highlights is perhaps best expressed by the book's subtitle: *Challenging Political Science*. As editors, our key to selecting texts and their thematic focus was their emphasis on Sartori as a debater and a polemicist. As we believe, this is what has been omitted from the many works about him, or to be more cautious in our statement, from the works about him that are available in English. Without doubt, Sartori was a great yet controversial scholar. Going against the mainstream was not just an occasional component of his work. It was his everyday practice. Sartori's sharp disputes with his peers, with his students and also with politicians are very much present in his scholarship. Challenging the mainstream was an inherent part of his political analysis. Sartori's adherence to the principles he set up for himself—an adherence that at times bordered on stubbornness—was manifest in all aspects of his academic and public work.

SARTORI'S LIFE AND WORK

Looking at his life in retrospect, one can identify patterns in Sartori's personality that already existed in his teenage years in Fascist Italy. Unlike many others, Sartori never joined the Fascist ranks and, risking the death penalty, even refused to join the Italian army. To avoid conscription in 1943, so the story goes, Sartori hid in a secret room in his family's house in Florence. This experience, dramatic in itself, significantly influenced Sartori's life. Hidden in that secret room, Sartori immersed himself in classical philosophy, reading works by Georg Wilhelm Friedrich Hegel, Immanuel Kant, Benedetto Croce, Giovanni Gentile and others. As Sartori reflected after the war, that experience was what actually kick-started his academic career, something that he had not planned for (and certainly not a career in philosophy, for that matter).

It was the postwar disruption of Italian academia—heavily infected with Fascism—and his knowledge of philosophy that brought Sartori his first academic position at the University of Florence. Paradoxically, it was not a position in political science. Sartori initially taught modern philosophy, and his first publications (including his dissertation on Hegel and Karl Marx (Sartori 1951) covered philosophy and political philosophy. Only in 1956 did Sartori teach his first course in political science. Sartori obtained his professorship (and a department of his own) in 1963, this time within sociology. Finally, in 1966, Sartori became the head of the Department of Political Science (and a professor in that discipline) at the University of Florence.

Why so late? Here we need to take into consideration that there was no political science—at least not as we understand the discipline today—in postwar Italy. As a field, Italian political science was not only highly compromised by Fascism but also existed only as a mixture of law, history, philosophy, sociology, economy, geography and other fields. As the reader may have guessed by now, Sartori had a completely different vision of political science. Hence, Sartori devoted his early years as a scholar to establishing political science as an independent discipline in Italy. According to him, political science needed to be an independent discipline, separate from philosophy or even political philosophy. Political science was to be an empirical science, characterised by a pragmatic and realistic approach to questions raised by society. In Sartori's view, political science examined politics in order to either confirm or form theories that then should be applicable in practice. It was to be worked out with variables, use a descriptive language and determine the relationship between means and goals. Such a concept of political science was utterly unthinkable in Italy at that time, and Sartori had to struggle hard for its acceptance.

Sartori not only newly defined political science in Italy, but he also contributed to its institutional growth by establishing the *Centro studi di politica comparata* as a 'youth training centre' for emerging scholars and the pivotal journal *Rivista Italiana di Scienza Politica*, serving as its editor until 2004. Above all, however, Sartori brought up a whole new generation of scholars who followed in his footsteps.

What might be interesting to us academics who feel we are barely surviving under the burden of the different administrative tasks our jobs include is that Sartori did not avoid administrative positions or organisational work. Between 1969 and 1971, Sartori was, for instance, Dean of the Faculty of Political Sciences at the University of Florence. (He once again manifested his willpower and fearlessness when he broke a strike of radical students.)

On top of that, Sartori also established the Department of Political and Social Science at the European University Institute in Florence.

In 1971, Sartori left for a year at Stanford University. The United States was not unknown territory for him. Sartori had first visited the United States in 1949 and later returned frequently, especially during the 1960s when he was a visiting professor at Harvard and Yale. What is more, Sartori maintained close contacts with the American Association for Political Science, taking part in its activities and establishing ties with a number of the leading figures of political science in the United States. Finally, in 1976, Sartori decided to leave Italy and immigrate to the United States. He first settled in Stanford, California, from where he moved to New York in 1979, becoming the Albert Schweitzer Professor in the Humanities at Columbia University.

While Sartori spent a considerable part of his professional life in the United States, he remained in isolation most of his time there. Although at first inspired by American empiricism, Sartori was never swayed by behaviouralism and did not fit into the American methodological mainstream. Instead, Sartori developed his own methodological system of social science. He became a 'European voice' on the American political science scene (Collier and Gerring 2009b, 2). In this volume, Sartori's life trajectory is examined in chapters 1 and 2.

Sartori returned to Italy in the 1990s, during a transition period from the 'first' to the 'second' Italian Republic. There he became a fierce commentator and an active participant in the public life of the country.

SARTORI AND POLITICS IN ITALY

When Sartori returned to Italy, he witnessed firsthand the failures of its traditional party system. Many experts, scholars of politics included, became members of various committees that aimed to reform the system, including the form of government, laws regulating the judiciary and the electoral system. Sartori quickly became the leading authority on political reform in Italy, and his position was bolstered as he began writing for the most widely read Italian daily, *Corriere della Sera*. Sartori's texts were often ironic and critical, and what is more, sharp-tongued. Sartori's columns were eventually gathered into two volumes (Sartori 2004a and 2006). Together with three of his other books (*Come sbagliare le riforme* [Sartori 1995a], *Seconda Repubblica? Sì, ma bene* [Sartori 1992] and *Il sultanato* [Sartori 2009]), they form the basis of his contribution to political reform in Italy. Around the same time, Sartori also became a popular TV personality, often commenting on the ongoing debate over constitutional reform.

It was not only that Sartori quickly gained a name for himself in academia. Sartori also enjoyed great respect from the Italian political establishment, both on the right and the left. In 1996, Antonio Maccanico even suggested Sartori as the Minister for Constitutional Reform (a position that Sartori declined to accept). Sartori was asked by Maccanico to draft a double-ballot electoral system based on the French model. In the end, neither that nor Sartori's own favoured semi-presidentialism ever saw the light of day. As a consequence, Sartori became a permanent and indefatigable opponent of political developments in the newly formed 'second' Italian Republic. True to his convictions, Sartori declined to take part in another attempt to reform the constitution, a refusal that cost him a position as a senator with lifelong tenure. Furthermore, Sartori fiercely rebuked the Italian version of majoritarian democracy proposed by Prime Ministers Silvio Berlusconi and Massimo D'Alema. Among many other such ideas proposed at the time, he rejected any notion of direct democracy that would limit the role of political institutions.

What we need to understand, however, is that while Sartori opposed the implementation of majoritarian democracy in Italy, he was not against it in principle. What he criticised was the wholesale transfer of the Westminster majoritarian model to the Italian political setting. He similarly rejected the then recently adopted mixed electoral system he called the *Mattarellum* because it would lead to an increased number of political parties, producing unstable, fragmented bipolar coalitions.

It might be interesting to note here that Sartori offered more than just a critique of the Italian political system and warned against dangers that all liberal democratic regimes might face. In his book *Homo videns* (Sartori 1997b), for instance, Sartori cautioned against the hollowing out of democracy by the rising influence of visual media (at that time represented by television). In his view, this trend would lead to an overabundance of information that ironically would cause citizens to become uninterested in politics. Fascinated by what they saw on television, such 'hypo-citizens' could be easily swayed by technocratic and populist leaders such as Silvio Berlusconi and Umberto Bossi.

At the beginning of the 2000s, Sartori focused on a new issue: multiculturalism. In his book *Pluralismo, multiculturalismo e estranei* (Sartori 2000b), Sartori openly attacked political correctness and criticised what he saw as a failing multicultural model. He returned to those issues in his subsequent books, the last of which was *La corsa verso il nulla. Dieci lezioni sulla nostra societa in pericolo* (Sartori 2015).

Giovanni Sartori was an uncompromising critic of political life—in Italy in particular. He criticised every aspect of the political developments of the 'second' Italian Republic, be they electoral reform, changes in the institutional order or attempts to create a 'strong premiership'. Later, Sartori subjected the more and more influential media and what he saw as a pervasive political correctness to his criticism. What needs to be stressed, however, is that his vibrant, cutting journalism was backed up by his firm grasp of logic. In his journalism, Sartori almost took pleasure in revealing the incompetence of his fellow academics, to say nothing of politicians. He never changed his opinions or convictions in exchange for personal gain or popularity. As will be shown, those convictions cost him wider influence over constitutional reform in Italy and a seat at the table of power as a senator. He was too stubborn to compromise his vision of liberal democracy and time proved him right. Sartori identified most of the flaws in the Italian political system years before they actually revealed themselves in full. The most striking example of this is the *Mattarellum* electoral system, praised by a majority of Italian scholars and politicians at the beginning. The *Mattarellum* had to be abandoned as nonfunctional in 2005, only to be replaced by an even less effective electoral system Sartori dubbed the *Porcellum* (a proportional system with a majority bonus). Chapters 3 and 4 offer a detailed account of Sartori's take on Italian politics.

SARTORI'S SCHOLARLY WORK

It was rather typical of Sartori that his scholarship was always linked to his life, his career path and his engagement in public matters. This connection clearly reflected Sartori's conviction that political science should be applicable in practice, or to put it otherwise, that the discipline of political science should be of use in the practical sphere of politics.

When it comes to Sartori as a political scientist, his scholarship can be divided into works that cover 1) political theory, 2) the methodology of social science, and 3) comparative politics. From his many works on political theory, Sartori is perhaps best known for his theory of democracy, a topic that he dealt with repeatedly. Writing first in Italian (Sartori 1957) and from the 1960s also in English (Sartori 1962), Sartori's most important work in this respect is *The Theory of Democracy Revisited* (Sartori 1987). Sartori became an advocate for the 'competitive theory of democracy', originally introduced by Josef (Joseph) Alois Schumpeter. In Sartori's view, that empirical (descriptive) theory best explains how democracy really works. Sartori gives it precedence over the theory of 'participatory democracy', which, according to him, fails to take into account the differences between ancient and modern democracies. As a critic of participatory democracy theory, Sartori understood that an empirical theory of democracy cannot answer every question. To understand democracy in all its complexity, we also need a normative (prescriptive) theory of democracy.

While *The Theory of Democracy Revisited* is certainly Sartori's best-known work when it comes to political theory, we should not forget about his texts on philosophy and political philosophy, especially those concerning

Hegel, Kant, Marx and Croce. Those texts, published during the early years of Sartori's academic career, are often overlooked. Many of them are still only available in Italian. We have included those works in our analysis of his systematic but now almost forgotten criticism of Marxism (chapter 8). Utilising his classical (philosophical) education, Sartori fully demonstrated his polemical talent in those texts.

Sartori's discussion of methodology is so multifarious and interwoven that we can speak of it as a whole system of social science methodology. What is characteristic of Sartori in this regard is that he was not interested in research techniques alone but in methodology as a way of thinking. At the foundation of Sartori's methodology of social science lie the 'concept formation' and 'misformation', both of which he closely connects to logical thinking and semantics. Sartori did not show any great respect for quantitative methods or mathematics as applied to political science. He believed that quantitative research has its place and role, but only after the relevant concepts have been formulated. Sartori's work on concepts and methods is perhaps the only area of his work that has already been scrutinised in detail (see, for example, Collier and Gerring 2009a). As a consequence, the methodological slice of Sartori's work receives only brief attention in our volume, mainly in chapter 2.

While Sartori's contributions to the theory of democracy and to methodology are essential reading for any social scientist, his works on comparative politics have had the most profound impact on political science. First and foremost, they include his publications on political parties, especially his typology of party systems (Sartori 1976), which is the most elaborate typology there is. His typology is based on interdependent criteria of fragmentation (number of parties) and polarisation (ideological distance between them). Sartori considers polarisation and not fragmentation to be the main explanatory variable of democratic party systems. For him, fragmentation merely determines the *format* of a party system. It is polarisation that determines its *mechanics*. That being said, a high degree of polarisation leads to polarised pluralism, which in Sartori's opinion endangers the functionality and, in extreme cases, the very existence of democracy. Polarised pluralism is—not surprisingly—a largely controversial form of democracy (based, among other things, on the often-criticised concept of anti-system parties). In our volume, Sartori's view of polarised pluralism is discussed in detail in chapter 6. Sartori's pivotal work on political parties, *Party and Party Systems* (Sartori 1976), dwells on a number of other concepts and theories. Together with *Les partis politiques* by Maurice Duverger (1951), it forms the foundation for contemporary research on parties and party systems. Another discussion of Sartori's party theory is included in chapter 5.

The second key work by Sartori about comparative politics is his *Comparative Constitutional Engineering* (1994). In that book Sartori scrutinised various democratic regimes and their functionality or dysfunctionality. It is a work that combines a thorough examination of politics with recommendations on how to proceed in practice. The book is his most openly polemical work (not counting Sartori's commentaries published in the press, that is). Here, among other things, Sartori questions Arend Lijphart's model of consensus democracy. His disagreements with Lijphart, to which Sartori returns in other works as well, are some of the most interesting and most important controversies raised in all of comparative political science. They had far-reaching theoretical and conceptual implications for the whole of political science and continue to resonate in the field. Needless to say, this was not an isolated dispute between the two authors. Given its importance, this dispute is introduced and examined in chapter 7.

ORGANISATION OF THIS VOLUME

This volume contains a selection of texts that reflect all the major aspects of Sartori's work (both scholarly and essayist in nature), as well as his life and public engagement. The eight chapters reflect upon all three major areas of his scholarship. The starting point of all chapters is an emphasis on the originality of Sartori's ideas and approaches, which often were controversial, challenging as they did not only the political science of the day but the social sciences as a whole and, last but not least, the prevailing public political discourse. Our volume reveals Sartori as an exceptionally original author writing on political theory, social science methodology and comparative politics. Sartori is also portrayed as a polemical essayist and publicist, an unshakably courageous commentator on politics and public life, especially in Italy.

The first chapter, authored by Gianfranco Pasquino, a student and later a colleague of Sartori, looks at Sartori's contributions to political science as a whole. In his thematically broad and intellectually deep examination, Pasquino draws examples from Sartori's study of democracy, his analysis of parties and party systems, his formulation of concepts and his ideas about comparative methods and constitutional engineering. Pasquino emphasises the fact that all these areas of Sartori's work are interconnected, forming a system the parts of which cannot be understood or examined in isolation. There is a close link between Sartori's scholarly work on the one hand and political practice on the other. To rephrase it, Sartori asserted that political science has to be applicable in practice and that political scientists must understand that theory cannot exist only for theory but must reflect the real political world. Otherwise, he contended, political science is worthless. That is why Pasquino, among others, pays so much attention to the relationship between Sartori's scholarship and his personal engagement in the Italian political debates of his time. That is also why Pasquino mentions Sartori's role in founding Italian political science, which has wider implications, not only in Italy. Pasquino's chapter highlights the major innovations introduced by Sartori and focuses on the differences between Sartori and his contemporaries, as well as certain inadequacies of political science today.

Michal Kubát's contribution follows in chapter 2, expanding on Pasquino's chapter by painting an intellectual portrait of Giovanni Sartori. How did Sartori's life experiences influence him as a scholar, and how did they impact Sartori's view of political science? As Kubát argues, there was indeed a very close connection between Sartori's life and how he perceived public matters. Like Pasquino, Kubát shows that Sartori's work, and indeed his conception of political science itself, cannot be separated or correctly understood without taking into account his life experience and his personality and character traits. Building on this argument, Kubát places great emphasis on Sartori's methodology, explaining how and why Sartori insisted on rigid concepts and terms, often setting himself up in opposition to the mainstream. Sartori is here portrayed as a solitary figure working in confrontation with the predominantly American political science, which paradoxically influenced him. As shown, Sartori criticised the excessive quantification of political science, which he believed was far too focused on the techniques of research, leading it into conflict with reality. Again there is Sartori's emphasis on the need for applicability in political science, a dictum which also spills over into other chapters, showing Sartori as an active observer and contributor to the vocabulary of Italian politics.

While the first two chapters of this volume offer complementary takes on the scope of Sartori's contributions to contemporary political science (especially in the case of his polemics against the predominant currents in the field), each of the following six chapters focuses on a specific angle of his life and work. Chapters 3 and 4 are very much 'Italian'. Martin Mejstřík and Oreste Massari show Sartori as an engaged and passionate intellectual who often commented on everyday politics in the Italy of the 1990s. Nevertheless, both chapters also show that Sartori's views, although they were addressed to Italy, have broader significance. Massari's chapter introduces Sartori's perspective on the creation of the 'second' Italian Republic. Mejstřík scrutinises the premises of Sartori's view that political science must be applicable in practice. What makes the two chapters interesting is that they both introduce a side of the 'legend' that has heretofore been little known outside of Italy. Both chapters are, however, largely pessimistic in their conclusions. They show that Sartori's advocacy for practicality in political science did not echo very much and that he did not succeed in convincing his colleagues of the need for an applicable political science. His insistence on transferring theory into political practice has not been supported by many political scientists, nor did it find much appeal in the broader community of scholars. Sartori was unable to succeed in influencing Italian politicians in the shaping of the reforms that they pursued in the course of the transition from the 'first' to the 'second' Italian Republic.

Chapters 5 and 6 shed light on another branch of Sartori's scholarship. His writings on political parties and party systems are Sartori's major contribution to comparative politics. Klaus von Beyme, Sartori's longtime peer, discusses three aspects of Sartori's party theory: party change, the sociology of parties and party organisation, and the policy outputs of parties in power and in coalitions. Unlike the mainstream of comparative politics, which prefers quantitative to qualitative methodology, Beyme offers convincing arguments for using the latter approach when it comes to the study of political parties. Beyme's chapter is broad in its scope and examines Sartori's contribution to the theory of political parties in its entirety. Maxmilián Strmiska expands on Beyme's essay, focusing on a specific type in Sartori's typology of party systems, 'polarised pluralism'. Strmiska uncovers Sartori's largely ignored arguments regarding the interaction between visible and invisible politics in polarised party politics. In here, Strmiska recounts Sartori's passionate defence of polarised pluralism, debate over which still continues today, to some extent. He also shows how Sartori tested the validity of all proposed typologies of party arrangements, including his own. While many might find Sartori's theory controversial, Strmiska shows that there is value in following his line of argumentation about polarised pluralism and its variants.

Whereas the earlier chapters scrutinise Sartori's works on comparative politics, in chapter 7 Miroslav Novák delves into not only comparative politics (constitutional engineering) but also political theory (democratic theory). In an original way typical of Novák, the author offers a new perspective on Sartori's critique of Lijphart's theory of consensus democracy and his (Lijphart's) contention that the consensus model of democracy is better for all countries. Novák clearly shows that Sartori's criticism of Lijphart benefits from his conceptual and terminological precision and his relentless search for the correct meaning of the terms he used. Similar terms can mean very different things (in this case, the terms *efficiency* and *effectiveness*). Terminological confusion can lead to incorrect conclusions, which is what happened to Lijphart. In the polemic between Sartori and Lijphart, we can see that for Sartori, conceptual rigour was not simply a kind of methodological formalism. Conceptualisation is what mattered most to the scholar.

Chapter 8, the final chapter of this book, is authored by Marek Bankowicz. It discusses Sartori's contributions to political theory. Bankowicz introduces Sartori's writings on Marx, which are almost forgotten today and remain available only to Italian speakers. Bankowicz shows that Sartori's critical analysis of Marxism was both conventional and innovative. Bankowicz argues that Sartori's most original contribution to political theory may be the insight that Marxism in its essence is not an egalitarian but ultimately a libertarian ideology. Sartori did not understand Marxism as an ideology of equality but as an ideology of liberty, though one often mistakenly defined and understood. Marx's cry for an alternative democracy and his vision of the definitive triumph of liberty that will bring about the ideal society and the end of history establish a basic link between him and Jean-Jacques Rousseau. Sartori considered Rousseau to be Marx's progenitor. While Rousseau may be the patron of those who aspire to supersede liberal democracy, Marx is the hero of those who reject liberal democracy altogether. Sartori points out that both of them, however, inspire their followers from far-reaching libertarian positions.

This last essay actually returns us to the beginning because, as shown earlier, Sartori from his youth was intrigued by Marx and other political philosophers, including Hegel and Croce. Today, it is Sartori who challenges scholars of politics. This volume is testimony to the value of revisiting the life and work of this 'giant of political science'—Giovanni Sartori.

Chapter One

Giovanni Sartori

A Giant of Political Science[1]

Gianfranco Pasquino

THE FOUNDATION OF POSTWAR ITALIAN POLITICAL SCIENCE AND MORE

Without the tireless, unconditional commitment to scholarship of Giovanni Sartori, political science would almost certainly not exist in Italy. Other important scholars, such as the economist Beniamino Andreatta, the political philosopher Norberto Bobbio, the scholar of administrative institutions Gianfranco Miglio, and Nicola Matteucci, a historian of political doctrines, collaborated with Sartori in various forms and ways. They worked together to reform the Faculty of Political Science at the University of Florence. However, the first powerful impulse for scholarship and for reform, which the others endorsed and elaborated upon, came from Sartori, as was clearly and effectively documented by Giorgio Sola (2005).

Sartori was not motivated solely by his research interests, which were partly influenced by his knowledge of what was happening on the other side of the Atlantic. Until the 1960s in Europe, there had been very little in the way of political science. From the very beginning, Sartori deliberately set himself two important long-term goals: first, to create a political culture in Italy that would challenge both Christian democratic culture and its communist counterpart, neither of which were inclined to a scientific and empirical study of politics; and second, to acquire and spread scientific knowledge applicable to politics (Sartori 1970c).

Sartori believed that political science had to use the comparative method to formulate its hypotheses, reach generalisations, produce theories and above all subject the results of its research to rigourous comparative control.

Sartori's (1970b) article 'Concept Misformation in Comparative Politics' is particularly fundamental to his scholarship and is still one of the most frequently and approvingly quoted articles in all of Italian political science. At about the time that article appeared, Sartori founded the *Rivista Italiana di Scienza Politica*, of which he was editor in chief until 2004.[2]

The political science Sartori desired, pursued and put into practice was never affected by his personal or party ambitions. It was meant to produce knowledge and elaborate on it in order to apply it to real life. To Sartori, political science had to find cognitive elements and formulate generalisations and probabilistic theories that could transform political reality and also that could be transformed, refined or even abandoned as necessary when they came into contact with that reality. It is precisely the exposure to this 'effectual' truth, to use the words of Niccolò Machiavelli, that serves as a test of the validity of the generalisations and the theories formulated by political scientists.

This is not the place to trace and criticise the evolution of Italian political science, whose promising beginnings were not followed by widespread and balanced growth (Pasquino, Regalia and Valbruzzi 2013). Among other things, with the exception of some well-taken criticisms he addressed to the blatant inadequacies and sheer lack of knowledge demonstrated by several other practitioners, Sartori and I hardly ever talked about the state of scholarship in the field. It is easy to see, however, that aside from a few scholars, the highly fragmented field of Italian political science is not at all following the road he clearly indicated and made practicable. The often sparse bibliographies of most Italian political scientists, on one hand, make us aware that practically none of them has interests applicable to reality. Many of them are trapped in one of the major pitfalls that Sartori attributed to American political science in the last twenty to thirty years: excessive specialisation. On the other hand, another flaw, excessive quantification, also exists in Italy. Only a few practitioners have fallen prey to it, perhaps because it requires skills that are rarely taught in Italian faculties of political science—none of which are currently called so, having almost all diffused, if not lost, their specific focus on the subject. It is certain, and ascertainable (by referring to their bibliographies and notes), that even when they are writing about some of his favourite topics, the vast majority of Italian political scientists know very little, perhaps almost nothing, about Sartori's political science. I would add that I am afraid (an understatement in the best British tradition) that those political scientists who more or less consciously reject the idea, the invitation and the fundamental precept that political science show its potential applicability to real-life situations thereby condemn their writings and themselves to irrelevance. Generalisations and probabilistic theories can only be tested by reference to political reality. They can also be falsified, which is Karl Popper's key methodological caveat. Because political events cannot be 'simulated' in a laboratory, applicability is the path political scientists ought to travel. Political science becomes relevant to the extent that it is capable of providing applicable knowledge. While political reformers may operate behind a veil of ignorance (John Rawls's fundamental lesson), institutional engineers should always formulate their generalisations with an eye open to applicability. This means that they must take into account the relationships among rules, behaviours, mechanisms and institutions and provide tentative evaluations of the possible or likely consequences of their proposals.[3]

I should not even need to add that Sartori never desired to impose the themes of his scholarly analyses upon others, nor was he derailed by his strong political preferences (liberalism, constitutionalism and the rule of law). Of course, he was highly aware of and interested in what was going on in the world and in the political science practiced by both his contemporaries and the great scholars of the past. What can be extracted from his very large scientific production is a clear and explicit preference for competitive democracy based on rules and institutions capable of producing political elites who represent the best of their society and the political system: 'Democracy should be a polyarchy of merit' (a quotation from his fundamental text on the matter, Sartori 1987, 169). Sartori's is a classic Schumpeterian view, which he enriches with his interpretations of all its components: electoral mechanisms, the choosing of teams of politicians and accountability. No synopsis can do justice to the elegance and conciseness of Schumpeter's theory or the sharpness of perspective with which Sartori rereads and enhances it. And no analysis of democracy can be complete and have meaning if it does not fully take into account what Schumpeter and Sartori have written.

NOT THE AUTHOR OF ONE SINGLE BOOK

As I have written several times (Pasquino 2009), Sartori was not the author of one sole book that he reworked over time. His research and writing interests embraced the entire field of political science. Comparisons of his writings often begin with his fundamental work *Democrazia e definizioni* (Sartori 1957). It contains numerous essays on the thoughts of some philosophers (Hegel, Marx, Kant and Croce) and also important essays on political representation and the structure of the state. It is possible for anyone who tackles science (even political science) to say that Sartori was climbing on the shoulders of giants, in the sense espoused by Robert Merton (1965) in his extraordinary book *On the Shoulders of Giants: A Shandean Postscript*. However, 'climbing' can only result in success for those who, like Sartori, read deeply and study the classics. Sartori lists both Carl Friedrich (1950) and Robert Dahl (1956) among his favourite authors who discuss democracy. In the Italian context of the 1950s, an intense debate on democracy arose between the great political philosopher Norberto Bobbio and the communists, who were seeking to gain respect and reduce concern about the consequences of their very possible rise to government.

I am unaware of any existing comparative readings of Bobbio's (1955) book *Politica e cultura* and Sartori's seminal book on democracy, but whoever does compare them would see that in different ways and different styles, both challenge communist thought and practice. This would be a fruitful exercise, and not only in terms of the history of Italian political science and the times. Sartori's approach is more scientific than Bobbio's, using words and constructing concepts according to a perspective he never abandoned. The Turin-born political philosopher Bobbio would continue to deal with the topic of democracy by publishing another book, *Il futuro della democrazia*, which earned unexpected success (Bobbio 1984). Bobbio's book has repeatedly been reprinted, a very rare phenomenon among renowned academics, recalling Sartori's (1987) own *The Theory of Democracy Revisited*. Bobbio raised some objections to what he considered Sartori's excessive 'realism'. On the occasion of Bobbio's death, Sartori's tribute ended with the words 'Norberto Bobbio was, and remains, the best of us all' (Sartori 2004b, 11). The two Italian giants of political philosophy and political science recognised each other's huge cultural contributions.

Sartori always insisted on the clear and unambiguous use of words (and sometimes as well on using them in an original and innovative way) and on clear concepts. The numerous essays he wrote over time to explain his fundamental concepts and his views on political phenomena were later collected in the precious volume *Elementi di teoria politica*, which has no equal. Sartori's book has been repeatedly reprinted by the publishing house il Mulino (the last time in 2016). For several years Sartori chaired the Committee on Conceptual and Terminological Analysis of the International Political Science Association, which produced a valuable book that he sponsored and edited: *Social Science Concepts: A Systematic Analysis* (Sartori 1984c). Unfortunately, the practical effect of that volume on political scientists has remained somewhat limited. Sartori did not have any successors, so the terminological and conceptual Babel quickly returned, with very negative effects on political analysis. Within the limits of our abilities, we tried to remedy the situation (Pasquino and Valbruzzi 2012), in a volume in which there is a valuable article contributed by Sartori (2012) himself.

As is the case everywhere, but in Italy more than anywhere else, the gusto for accuracy and conceptual clarity has been lost. I often told Sartori that he had lost his praiseworthy battle over concepts and that consequently the ability of political science to formulate 'probabilistic' generalisations and theories was sharply curtailed. He hurriedly replied that all theories have to be fully characterised by both scientificity and intersubjectivity. Those who do not use the same language and concepts with precise and unambiguous meaning cannot, of course, communicate with other scholars in a valid or convincing way. I reminded Sartori that since 1993 he had himself expressed increasing dissatisfaction with American political science for what he defined as its 'excesses' of specialisation and quantification, which condemn it to irrelevance and sterility (Sartori 1997a). Occasionally, especially when I am invited to hold a conference on a particular subject, I take into my hands the collection of Sartori's works, *Elementi di teoria politica*, because from ideology to public opinion, from constitutions to electoral systems, from liberalism to representation, all are 'entries' in that unsurpassed volume. I always get what I want: a light that illuminates the past—where you find the contributions of the 'giants' who constructed the fundamental concepts of political science—and a path forward into the future. I really cannot restrain myself from saying it: Sartori provides a light that dispels the superficiality, the approximation and the 'posttruth' of our contemporaries.

SARTORI'S POLITICAL SCIENCE AND THE ITALIAN CASE

In the post–World War II period there were no giants in the field of Italian political science on whose shoulders to climb. There were no particularly important studies in political science. In history, yes, there was the excellent volume by Federico Chabod (1961), which deserves to be mentioned. In 1967, however, a volume with absolutely provocative content appeared as part of a broader research effort (Galli and Prandi 1968). It was titled *Il bipartitismo imperfetto. Comunisti e democristiani in Italia* (Galli 1967). A year earlier, Sartori had published a fundamental chapter outlining a clear comparative approach, in which the Italian party system was only one example of what he termed 'polarised pluralism' (Sartori 1966a). Sartori denied that the Italian party system could at its root be considered a variant of a two-party system. No, there were not two parties only in Italy. Above all, the dynamic was not one of common, periodical rotation of the parties in power. Quite the contrary: the Italian party system was an obvious example of a multiparty system in which there was an imminent risk that the two extremist parties, the neofascists, and especially the communists, would weaken and hollow out the centre, thus collapsing the entire political system. Sartori collected his scholarly, but nonetheless sharp and biting, articles on the Italian situation in a thick volume (Sartori 1982).

Sartori's ideal democracy was a 'democracy of parties', built on the awareness that parties are essential to democracy and that democracy needs competition between at least two parties that must offer alternatives to voters. What kind of competition, how many parties and what alternatives should be on offer are all topics that Sartori explored, outlined, elaborated upon and interpreted in an original, consistent, comparative way. As is often the case with Italian academics, the beginnings of his scholarship date back to his lecture notes, that is, the gathering of his notes from his university classes, which were published in a volume in 1965. A few years later, preceded by several important articles, chapters and essays (Sartori 1968a; 1969; 1970d), each of which deserves to be analysed in itself, his fundamental book *Party and Party Systems* (Sartori 1976) saw the light. Even twenty years after its publication, the American Political Science Association awarded this book a prize as a still outstanding text. Some Italian political scientists, who learned so much from that text, appropriately celebrated it on the fortieth anniversary of its publication (Pasquino 2016).

Prior to Sartori, political parties had always quite rightly been one of the central, if not the most important, objects of study in political science (one must see the studies by Duverger 1951; Neumann 1956; Lipset and Rokkan 1967). However, most important to remember, as far as the analysis of party systems is concerned, is that much remained to be done on the classification of parties and the arrangements for their competition. Sartori's decisive contribution was his absolutely original classification of party systems. He not only counted the number of parties (one must know how to 'count' and, as was the main point of Sartori's highly original contribution, to identify 'the parties that count'), but he also discussed the dynamics of competition between parties that have coalition potential and parties that have only blackmail potential. I fear, however, that Sartori's classification has not yet been sufficiently appreciated nor adequately used, even in the best studies in the field—and I consider Mair (1997) and Karvonen and Kuhnle (2001) to be among the best. When we have more than twice as many competing party systems as in Sartori's time, it would be interesting to test what Sartori modestly defined as his 'framework for analysis' (which is the subtitle of his book).

Having returned to Italy after more than twenty years of experience in the United States, Sartori was forced to deal again with Italian politics. He did so with pleasure, never forgetting his knowledge of political science nor his comparative perspective in his many journal articles (Sartori 2004a; 2006). The foundations of his critical appraisals of poorly formulated reforms and his proposals for better reforms are clearly stated and argued in his *Comparative Constitutional Engineering* (Sartori 1994, in Italian Sartori 1995b). Some claim that one cannot expect Italian commentators and journalists to know Sartori's scientific production—but why not? Those who write about electoral and constitutional reforms in Italy and elsewhere have three duties: first, to explore Sartori's assessments of Italian electoral and institutional reforms; second, to go beyond simplistic references to Sartori as the inventor of the mocking terms *Mattarellum* and *Porcellum*; and third, to deal with his specific proposals. With those two well-fitting and derisive Latin sobriquets, Sartori intended to point out (and brilliantly succeeded in doing so) the disadvantages of the electoral law of 1993–1994, for which the Christian Democrat Sergio Mattarella (elected in 2015 to the presidency of the Italian Republic) was the rapporteur. Sartori also condemned the manipulations of the vote by the *Porcellum* (formulated by Senator Calderoli of the Northern League), which had the primary goal of giving an advantage to the centre-right coalition led by Berlusconi.

What of course counts much more than those derogatory Latinisms, though they still stick, is the content of Sartori's substantial criticism of those two electoral systems. I will say more about this shortly. Here I will merely point out first that the Italian political system is still waiting for a decent electoral law. Second, if the *Mattarellum* were to be revived, it would have to be redefined so as to avoid the drawbacks identified by Sartori, in particular, those that facilitate and perpetuate party fragmentation. Sartori saw nothing worth saving in the case of the *Porcellum*, however. His worries about how little attention politicians devoted to his criticisms and proposals for reform were not so much derived from a desire to obtain recognition of his personal merits. They sprang from his acute awareness that a political system such as the Italian one, with its persistent electoral and institutional problems, would never be able to work satisfactorily. He knew also that a bad electoral law could never contribute to the needed restructuring of the party system.

Just as a more or less hidden struggle is ongoing for an electoral law that may most benefit those who get to draft it and most disadvantage their opponents, it is worth remembering that Sartori never argued in these particular terms. Also, Sartori's comparative perspective was totally opposed to the views of those who were telling the fable that the Italian system was an anomaly that could even be considered to be 'positive'. He warned against what should not be done and pointed out solutions, eventually reaching a well-argued conclusion that the preferable electoral law would mandate a two-round system such as exists in France. He supported a constitutional reform establishing single-member constituencies and a semi-presidential regime similar to that of the French Fifth Republic (a solution that I strongly agree with). In order to prevent a party and its candidate list from being excluded from the second round of voting by a nationwide threshold for participation, Sartori suggested the possibility of allowing access to the second round to the first four candidates in each single-member constituency. That solution was ingenious. It did not invalidate all the good aspects of a second round of voting: more opportunities given to voters, more information available to candidates and parties, a stimulus to formation of coalitions competing to govern and 'punishment' for those who do not seek and find allies.

I have already pointed out that in the highly confused Italian debate on electoral reform (which was at times cynically manipulated by its shrewdest participants), Sartori has entered history as the one who coined the terms

Mattarellum and *Porcellum*. The scientific origin of those terms deserves to be explored. A worthwhile comparative scientific analysis stands behind those two sarcastic expressions. They stigmatize two electoral laws, both of which had several drawbacks (the *Porcellum* more so than the *Mattarellum*), especially in terms of respecting the electorate's wishes and increasing the accountability of those elected. Sartori's opposition to the *Mattarellum* was based precisely on his awareness that instead of reducing or at least limiting party fragmentation, that electoral law rewarded and encouraged it. 'Geographically concentrated' minorities, which escape the lenses of most electoral system scholars, are often in a position to obstruct two-party competition, and even bipolarism, which is the competition between two coalitions that are credible candidates to govern. The purpose and the substance of Sartori's criticisms regularly and deliberately result in a series of probabilistic predictions made with reference to existing conditions and specific proposals for change. Over forty years ago, Sartori was already perfectly aware of the importance of 'context', to which some American scholars have only just recently turned their attention (see Htun and Powell 2013). From my vantage point as one of Sartori's students, I think I can add that he would not have accepted a revival of the *Mattarellum* unless it was appropriately modified.

Politicians regularly make the imperious request that all reformers who do not accept the hand (or rather the finger) they are dealt, and who criticise them, should formulate their own proposals. Sartori's ingenious proposal is easy to retrieve from his works on the subject of electoral engineering—and it is not to disadvantage anyone in the starting blocks. He advocates a French-style two-round system in single-member constituencies but with an important and highly interesting variant for access to the second round, a second round that it is preferable not to call a run-off. In fact, in the second round of French parliamentary elections there is a possibility, not an obligation or anything automatic, of more than two candidates going to the second round. This is the case in about three-quarters of the electoral constituencies. I suggest that it is actually a run-off when only two candidates are allowed to advance to the second round, as is the case in the French presidential elections. This has very different consequences for electoral campaigns, guidelines and voting behaviour. Instead of setting a nationwide percentage threshold for access to the second round of voting, Sartori suggested that in all single-member constituencies the first four candidates should be allowed to participate in the second round. Thus, from time to time and place to place, where there are popular local candidates who are good campaigners and can represent a specific electorate, they and their parties would have an opportunity to compete against candidates of parties that are much stronger nationally.

Sartori would be more than surprised to hear that the existence of three poles (in Italy, presumably the fractured centre-right, the Democratic Party and the Five Star Movement) obliges the enactment of an electoral law providing for proportional representation in some unspecified form. Of course, it is understandable that the Italian parties will try any trick to obtain an electoral law that gives them some advantage or that, at least at first sight, does not disadvantage them. History shows that myopic politicians are very likely to make mistakes. However, the substantial literature on electoral systems focuses on another far more important phenomenon. Many scholars have repeatedly questioned the influence of electoral systems on party systems, starting with Maurice Duverger. They have come up with many answers, though not always convincing ones. Sartori too offered some nuanced answers, revisiting Duverger and correcting his analysis in part. Sartori in turn has been 'corrected' in many respects. For a review, I would recommend reading the brief, but very dense, article by Domenico Fisichella (2014).

It is certain that Sartori would examine both the strength of the Italian parties and that of the Italian party system before arguing for one electoral system that would be appropriate for Italy. He did so almost fifty years ago, in a remarkable chapter that did not get the attention it deserved (Sartori 1968a). I am convinced that he would express his well-documented preference for a 'constraining' electoral system that would prevent the (further) fragmentation of the Italian party system and encourage the formation of coalitions. Finally, he would state, in a loud and stinging voice, that whichever direction you want to go, you must pay close attention to comparisons, exploring and evaluating how various electoral laws have worked elsewhere, and along with which party systems. To make comparisons, you do not have to call in lawyers, even those of the level of the Constitutional Court, because they do not have sufficient knowledge of the functioning of political systems. They know even less about how parties actually work and how voters behave, depending on the electoral systems in which they vote. The most classic distinction is between a sincere vote and a strategic vote. When there are two rounds of voting, even in Italy, the voter has the maximum opportunity to express his or her choice. Electoral laws are a field of research, analysis and intervention eminently suited to political scientists.

After denying for too long the importance of the electoral system to the functioning and transformation of the party and political systems, many Italian commentators and scholars have ended up attributing absolute and decisive importance to electoral systems. Exaggeration follows exaggeration. It is likely that the Italian Parliament will be unable to approve anything better than a proportional electoral law without any majority bonus.[4] Some Italian political commentators have warned that the spectre of Weimar is lurking about like Marx's communism, not in Europe but in Italy. It is haunting almost exclusively newspaper editorial offices and the salons attended by a mix of journalists, politicians and intellectuals of various types, who are certainly unenlightened and unfamiliar with knowledge of comparative systems.

Sartori also dealt with the Weimar Republic comparatively, from the point of view of its structure and the functioning of its party system. Weimar was Sartori's first example of polarised pluralism. The other cases of polarised pluralism included in Sartori's analytical framework were the Spanish Second Republic (1931–1936), the Fourth French Republic (1946–1958), Chile under Frei and Allende (1964–1973) and the Italian Republic (1946–1992). All of these political systems were characterised by extreme multiparty systems and by the existence of two anti-system opposition parties. In the case of Weimar these were the Stalinist communists and the National Socialists. A great, indeed insurmountable, ideological distance separates the parties in each system. Alternation in power is impossible, and extremist parties attempt to empty the centre (represented in Weimar by the Social Democrats) of its power and supporters.

I am here neglecting the international context of the times, which was extraordinarily different from that of the present. Chapters in the volume edited by Linz and Stepan (1978) very convincingly document how important, if not decisive, the international context is to understand the failure of unstable, unconsolidated democracies. Not even the least prepared or the most distracted observer can fail to notice the qualitative differences between the Weimar party system in Germany and that of contemporary Italy. Although the Five Star Movement is in no way similar to the Nazis, it is certainly possible to consider it an anti-system actor, that is, as defined by Sartori, an actor that would change the system if that is possible. But it seems absurd to suggest that the direct democracy that Five Star Movement MPs, supporters and voters would like to implement in place of the shaky representative democracy currently in existence is similar to the tragedy of Weimar, either in its modalities or its presumed consequence, the collapse of the current regime. At the same time, to build (with difficulty) a direct democracy, it is essential to know representative democracy, which does not exactly seem to be in the cultural heritage of the Five Star Movement. The prophets who worry that Weimar's destiny is an ingredient of the Italian sauce must understand the fundamentals of political representation, which include a basic requirement for the absence of imperative mandates. They must also support electoral laws that guarantee democracy in the best possible way. Obviously, adequate political representation is impossible if the electoral system is based on blocked lists, as in the so-called *Porcellum*, or on blocked top candidates, as in the so-called *Italicum*. This is also true of the electoral law formulated by the Renzi government, several features of which were declared unconstitutional by the Italian Constitutional Court. I have highlighted its very serious drawbacks (Pasquino 2015).

Because they are the least-known elements of his works outside of Italy, I have explained Sartori's critique of some aspects of the Italian political system at length, in particular, the party system and the electoral laws, which Sartori's writings allow us to better understand, evaluate and criticise from a comparative point of view. His work is most useful, indeed indispensable, to those who want to understand Sartori's reformist goals and his conception of political science as a science with applicability to the real world. One issue of the review *ParadoXa*, titled 'La Repubblica di Sartori' (2014), contains several important analyses and some excellent syntheses of the central aspects of his contributions to the literature on political representation, to explaining party-based competition and to the search for electoral laws that give effective power to voters. However, at least in Italy, the time of the 'Republic of Sartori' is still yet to come.

IS IT POSSIBLE TO GO BEYOND SARTORI, AND IF SO, HOW?

One can read and interpret more or less deeply only one text at a time from an author. In this chapter, I have prioritized Sartori's studies and articles dedicated to Italian politics for two reasons. First, because they are not easily accessible to those who do not know the Italian language and political system. Second, because they demonstrate both the importance of the comparative method and the possibility of applying political science to real-world situations. Of course, Sartori was involved in a large, lively and exciting international circle, in which he was a very active presence and a very prolific author. Sartori himself listed a number of great scholars whom he considered lifelong friends: Marty Lipset, Juan Linz, Stein Rokkan, Mattei Dogan, Hans Daalder and S. N. Eisenstadt, in addition to Gabriel A. Almond and Robert A. Dahl, for both of whom he expressed his greatest appreciation as scientists (Sartori 1997a, 95–97). I have personally met all the scholars he mentions, though naturally in a far less personal way than Sartori. I have diligently read almost all of what they wrote. That is why I have often asked myself what influence those scholars had on Sartori, and Sartori on them.

On the one hand, the outcome of my research turned out to be extraordinarily complicated. If I may be permitted to write the following, it is impossible to read all the works Sartori himself read and trace all of his many citations. However, it is enough to consider his most important predecessors' texts to realise immediately that Sartori regularly went beyond their theories. We must mention Schumpeter's competitive theory of democracy in that regard, on which Sartori relied. He integrated and completed it with a crucial element he derived from Carl J. Friedrich: 'anticipated reactions'. Politicians want to be reelected. For this reason, immediately after winning an election, they try to keep in tune with their electorate. They also constantly try to reconstitute their winning formula by establishing a relationship of representation and accountability with the voters. This is precisely what hasty readers and critics of Schumpeter's theory, the so-called participationists (whom Sartori duly criticised in *The Theory of Democracy Revisited*) cannot understand. Recently, the word and the challenge have passed to the 'deliberationists', but their results do not yet seem satisfactory and rewarding to me. Antonio Floridia (2017) has tried to deal very fairly with Sartori's ideas and those who criticised him.

It remains necessary, not only from the point of view of the history of ideas and the ways in which political science is progressing, to try to reconstruct the path Sartori took in the writing of his books. What was there before him? What was the state of knowledge? What did he read and use (and, above all, what did he neglect)? In short, how great was his originality? My research was facilitated only in part by the fact that Sartori, as he himself said is an imperative for those who want to engage in scientific work, had 'his bibliography in order'. He actually read, seriously considered, evaluated and criticised everything written before him on every subject with which he dealt. I will give but one example which, given its absolute relevance, seems decisive to me: Sartori's analysis of parties, party systems and their classification. I have already mentioned his truly unsurpassed innovation of 'counting the parties that count' and then formulating and expounding the criteria of relevance and using them for comparative analysis. All previous analyses and classifications were limited and did not go beyond simple numerical calculations that were at times severely misleading. Sartori added two qualitative criteria to the mix: coalition potential and blackmail power. He also suggested the criteria that can lead to successful operationalization of both those characteristics. Finally, even with knowledge of the sources of Sartori's theories, little or nothing of what is found in *Comparative Constitutional Engineering* can be fully and deeply understood, or appropriately implemented, by anyone who does not know about Sartori's reflections on the constitution and liberalism (Sartori 1962), on the separation of powers and checks and balances and additionally on the classification of party systems and their impact on parliaments and governments.

This point is worthy of elaboration. Quotations are often used by scholars perfunctorily and at random, in some cases to signal that a writer belongs to a specific school of political science or, as Gabriel Almond (1990) wrote, to a narrow sect. This was not Sartori's style. His footnotes always served the purpose of better clarifying a particular concept, sentence or comment. His quotations always contained precise references to the pages of the articles, chapters and books he referred to. Moreover, he always explained why he agreed with whom and about what. Otherwise, he argued at length when he disagreed. It is too often stated that what really matters is asking good questions. Sartori never confined himself simply to asking good questions, that is, questions about political phenomena that beg explanation. On the contrary, he was always suggesting working hypotheses in an attempt to find alternative solutions and formulate probable outcomes. In order to do all this in a satisfactory way, his articles, essays and books took into consideration the entire literature available at the time they were written. They have become indispensable documents of the times, but above all they are building blocks on which scholarly work continues to construct new theories.

CONCLUSION

In conclusion, the set of innovations that Sartori introduced into political science is remarkable in terms of methods (especially the required elements of solid comparative analysis) and in terms of substance in the three fields of his scientific research and production. Sartori was a full-fledged political scientist. His most fundamental lesson is that democracy, parties and institutions are closely connected. They make up a system. They must always be analysed from a comparative perspective. Whenever there is a change in one element, it will affect the other two. Democracy, parties and institutions can, and sometimes must, be reformed to improve their functioning, which will improve the lives of citizens in turn. Good, relevant political science cannot exist when and where its practitioners do not have adequate knowledge of institutions and parties (and about what makes for a democratic regime). Nor can it exist when political scientists do not believe that their findings and their theories have real-world applicability. All that being said, there are many scholars who devote themselves to different, diverse themes and phenomena and to specific aspects of each topic. But not even those who can see the trees will be able to see the forest if, to conclude with a sentence I consider particularly suggestive and effective,[5] they have not managed to climb onto the shoulders of the giant of political science that Giovanni Sartori most certainly was. Because of the intellectual and scholarly stature of Sartori, most certainly a giant, the climbing will not at all be easy, but it will be immensely rewarding.

NOTES

1. This chapter is a significantly revised and considerably enlarged version of a piece that was originally published in Italian in the quarterly journal *Nuova Antologia*, April–June 2017.

2. I was honoured to be the *Review*'s chief editor for the first seven years of its existence and co-editor from 2001 to 2004.

3. Marco Valbruzzi suggested this rule to me some time ago. It is much worth pursuing. I have offered more than a preliminary assessment in the article 'Political Science for What? Giovanni Sartori's Scholarly Answer' (Pasquino 2013a). More recently, I came across the *Cambridge Handbook of Experimental Political Science* (Druckman et al. 2011), a useful collection of articles and experiments. Perhaps because Druckman's handbook is somewhat

wanting in terms of conceptualisation, it does not directly tackle the issue of applicability of political science knowledge, no matter how acquired.

4. Incidentally, electoral laws mandating proportional representation have been in effect for more than a century in all European democracies that have not been subject to authoritarian interruptions.

5. Curiously, or better, ludicrously, in a joint communiqué on the occasion of his death, the president of the Italian Political Science Association, SISP (*Società Italiana di Scienza Politica*), which was founded by Sartori, and the editors of the *Rivista Italiana di Scienza Politica*, also founded in 1971 by Sartori and then donated by him to the SISP in 2004, defined Sartori as '*probably* the best Italian political scientist' (italics mine). I suppose many are anxiously waiting to know who the other candidates are for the title of 'best Italian political scientist'. In the meantime, my evaluation is that Sartori belongs to a small group of the five or six most outstanding political scientists of the twentieth century.

Chapter Two

An Italian in New York, an Alien to Political Science?

An Intellectual Portrait of Giovanni Sartori[1]

Michal Kubát

This chapter offers a brief intellectual portrait of Sartori with an emphasis on the specifics of his broad body of work, which distances him from the mainstream of contemporary political science (especially comparative politics). I will analyse these particular features of his work with a focus on Sartori's 'methodological writings', which the reader cannot (and should not) view as research techniques but rather the *logos*—a way of thinking. For Sartori was not just a comparative political scientist, as it may seem at first glance; he himself placed emphasis on this fact:

> In truth, I am only a part-time comparativist. My work can be divided in three slices: (1) straightforward political theory; (2) methodological writings . . . ; and (3) comparative politics proper. (Sartori 1997a, 95)

Although he studied many different issues, all his work has a single 'backbone' (Sartori 1997a, 95) determined by his philosophical roots and theoretical and methodological conscience. His work includes a firm conviction about how political science should look, what the political scientist's mission is and what we should think of when we hear the term 'politics'. Sartori's conception of 'politics' and 'political science', of course, are closely connected not just with his work in and of itself but also with the circumstances of his life. After all, he himself very aptly titled his short autobiography 'Chance, Luck and Stubbornness' (Sartori 1997a, 93–100).

THE PHILOSOPHICAL UNDERPINNINGS OF SARTORI'S WORK

Giovanni Sartori spent his childhood and young adulthood in Italy during the era of fascism. In October 1943, he received a draft card for the army of the Republic of Salò. Sartori decided not to report to the army, regardless of the risk of death by firing squad, and hid until liberation in August 1944. At first, he stayed in a villa near Florence; from there, however, he had to escape through the meadows to avoid the Germans, who were carrying out home searches in the area. He finally took refuge in a 'secret room' in his grandparents' home in Florence (Truzzi 2014). What is there to do when you are spending ten months or so in hiding and cannot be seen by anyone? Sartori's solution was *consolatione philosophiae* (Sartori 1997a, 93). He read philosophical texts, mainly Hegel, Kant, Benedetto Croce and Giovanni Gentile. Above all, the unintelligible Hegel proved to be a tough nut to crack. As Sartori himself remembered,

> It took me one day to read ten, at most fifteen pages of Hegel. At the end of the day I was definitely exhausted and ready for bed. (Sartori 1997a, 93)

This exhausting philosophical reading, however, had far-reaching consequences. On the one hand, it kept him busy while in hiding until the end of the war. Mainly, though, it caused Sartori to set off on an academic career after the war. Although he did not want to be a philosopher and did not even plan a career as a university professor, the postwar academic breakdown, when 'the university was almost like a desert; most of the professors were investigated for collaboration with fascism' (Truzzi 2014), and his knowledge of philosophy (Hegel) provided him with his first academic position at the Department of State Law under Professor Pompeo Biondi. Sartori's first book-length publications and university textbooks were devoted to philosophy and political philosophy: to Hegel (Sartori 1951), Kant (Sartori 1953) and Croce (Sartori 1955).[2]

Sartori later made use of his philosophical underpinnings in many works. He created a critique of Marxism that is today relatively poorly known but is nonetheless systematic and well thought out.[3] He also made use of his philosophical education in his study of democracy. Sartori (1957; 1965; 1987; 1993; 2008) wrote many books on the theory of democracy, all republished many times over. These books are based on a combination of historical, conceptual, empirical and theoretical approaches (Pasquino 2009, 170). Due in part to his knowledge of political philosophy, Sartori recognised the crucial significance of the distinction between ideal and real democracy (in this he was also influenced by Robert A. Dahl [1956]). On one side is the mandate theory of democracy, which can be orthodox or classical; on the other side is the competitive theory of democracy, founded by Joseph A. Schumpeter (1942). Sartori became one of the main representatives of Schumpeter's competitive theory of democracy, which is descriptive and, as such, explains how democracy really works.[4] On the other hand, he did not entirely reject the mandate theory of democracy and acknowledged its prescriptive validity. The competitive theory of democracy 'does not attempt to replace it. It is rather an extension and completion of it' (Sartori 1965, 127).

'THERE WAS NO POLITICAL SCIENCE IN ITALY BEFORE GIOVANNI SARTORI'

Sartori's student and collaborator Gianfranco Pasquino (2009, 167) used these words to begin his brief essay on Sartori's work. Although Italy of course did have a tradition of 'the science of politics' or 'the study of politics', until the 1950s, there was no political science as we understand it today as a distinct and institutionalized field of science and study. Sergio Panunzio in Perugia founded the first faculty of political sciences in 1925. The Faculty of Political Sciences in Florence was started in 1938, and other similar faculties were opened later still (Sola 2005, 31–32). As paradoxical as it may sound, though, there was no political science in these schools of political science.[5] The 'political sciences' (in the plural) comprised law, history, economics, statistics, geography and philosophy. Later, Sartori somewhat ironically recalled:

> How can we have political sciences in the plural without a political science in the singular that explains what all the rest is about? (Sartori 1997a, 95)

Sartori thus first had to teach the history of modern philosophy, beginning in 1950. He only began his first course in political science in Florence in 1956, and even then it was over the objection of his supervisor, philosopher Carlo Antoni—a student of Croce's—who was responsible for the subject within the faculty (Sola 2005, 34–35). In 1963, he received his department—a Department of Sociology, of course—and only became the chair of the Department of Political Science in 1966.[6]

At last, then, Giovanni Sartori had won the struggle for institutional recognition of political science in Italy. However, he also—above all else, really—needed to somehow capture political science, define it. Sartori's conception of political science must be understood in the context of the time and place in which he lived. This conception, after all, arose from a rejection of the Italian understanding of the study of politics. The Italian tradition of the 'science of politics' was completely different from political science as understood by Sartori. Giorgio Sola (2005, 57) correctly pointed out that Sartori's political science was *ex novo*—that is, distinct from the past of Italian 'political science'[7] represented especially by Gaetano Mosca (1953)[8] and his *Ele-*

menti di scienza politica from 1896. Sartori, of course, did not invent political science as such; he 'merely' gave it a new meaning.

According to Sartori, political science should above all be an empirical science distinguished by a pragmatic, realistic (and not emotional) approach—of course, in the Italian context of the time, in which empiricism was perceived as 'derogatory' (Sartori 1997a, 96), this was an extremely bold declaration. Political science should use the study of politics as a means for corroborating or creating a theory that is to be applicable in practice (Sartori 1979). Furthermore, political science works with variables, makes use of descriptive language and establishes a relationship between means and ends. Beginning with Machiavelli—who, of course, was neither a philosopher nor a scientist—politics has been independent (of ethics, morality, religion, economics, etc.)—that is, it follows its own rules—and is self-sufficient (autarkic) in the sense that it can explain itself (Sartori 1973b). Metaphorically, political science should have similar qualities as well. It must be an independent science, and it cannot be philosophy or political philosophy, especially from a methodological viewpoint (Sartori 1974b).

Political science should not be sociology—or rather the situation is more complicated because Sartori (1969), as is well known, distinguished between the sociology of politics and political sociology. While the sociology of politics is a part of sociology, just like, say, the sociology of religion or the sociology of the media, political sociology is a field that crosses the boundaries between disciplines and is linked with political science (as it is a part of both sociology and political science); it is, in Sartori's (1969, 197) words, 'an inter-disciplinary hybrid'. Political sociology understands, to put it simply, political actors (for example, a political system) as independent variables, while the sociology of politics does the opposite. The sociology of politics is thus a sort of 'sociological reduction of politics'; that is, a reduction that serves to clarify political phenomena through sociological, and thus nonpolitical, variables.[9]

Given that Sartori rejected the Italian tradition of political science, what did he use as a foundation? Sartori stated that he was an autodidact who did not have teachers and had to rely on himself, on his own judgement (Sartori 1997a, 95). Things were not so bad, though; after all, there was an environment in which he could look for inspiration: American political science. Sartori first spent time in the United States in 1949–1950 and returned repeatedly thereafter. As he himself stated, 'My understanding of political science undoubtedly bore an American imprint' (Sartori 1997a, 96). In addition to Sartori's stays in the United States, he was strongly influenced by the International Political Science Association (IPSA), in whose actions he participated and in which he came to know many classic figures of contemporary political science, who later became his lifelong friends (G. Almond, H. Daalder, M. Dogan, S. N. Eisenstadt, J. J. Linz, S. M. Lipset and S. Rokkan).

Above all, he recalled the Committee for Political Sociology where, among other things, he promoted his distinction, described earlier, between political sociology and the sociology of politics (Sartori 1997a, 100). Also important for Sartori were the many IPSA conferences in which he participated, including in Italy (for example, the IPSA Teaching and Research in Comparative Government roundtable that took place in April 1954 in Florence).

ITALIAN IN NEW YORK

As previously mentioned, Giovanni Sartori first visited the United States in 1949. He regularly returned there in the 1960s as a visiting professor (Harvard, Yale). However, he spent the turbulent years around the end of that decade as dean of his faculty in Florence (1969–1971). In 1971, tired out after three years of 'battles',[10] he left for a year at Stanford. Finally, in 1976, he decided to leave Italy for good and moved to the United States. He first landed at Stanford, where a professorship had become available upon Gabriel Almond's retirement. In 1979 he moved to New York, where he became Albert Schweitzer Professor in the Humanities at Columbia University and, after 1994, a professor emeritus.

Why did Sartori decide to leave Italy? Gianfranco Pasquino (2009, 168) claims that he left because he was tired of constant clashes with university bureaucracy and was altogether disgusted with the Italian university system. Sartori (1997a, 98) himself diplomatically gave somewhat different reasons. After more than a quarter of a century in Florence, he felt that he had done what he could in Italy and that he no longer had anything new to offer Italian political science. In addition, a number of his students had become fully established political scientists in several Italian universities, and Italian political science could thus run its own course independently without his guardianship. He wanted to focus on himself, on his own academic career. Similarly, Giorgio Sola (2005, 63) wrote that Sartori wanted to gain new experiences abroad and also had the sense that he had achieved his goal in Italy: political science as an advanced, legitimate and autonomous field.

Giovanni Sartori thus made his way to a country whose political science had had a strong influence on him from the beginning. It would seem that he had a dazzling career ahead of him. Well, yes and no. On the one hand, he got extremely prestigious positions at the best universities. He published his most influential works in the United States. On the other hand, he never became a part of the mainstream of American political science. He always stood at a distance. He resembled the character in the famous British musician Sting's 1987 hit 'Englishman in New York' who, as 'a legal alien', prefers tea to coffee, makes his toast in a different way and speaks with a foreign accent. Sartori was similar in this; only the nationality was different:

not 'Englishman in New York' but 'Italian in New York'. He was very much aware of this and years later recollected that his 'work has never made a splash on American soil' (Sartori 1997a, 99). Juan Linz had a similar view, saying,

> I'm not sure, but I have the impression that while he was in the United States, Sartori did not have much impact on the people who worked with him compared to his great impact on a whole generation of Italian scholars. (Linz 2007, 199)

In their recollections, his students also said that the well-liked but at the same time somewhat feared Sartori 'was not your typical university professor in the United States' (Skach et al. 2009, 343).[11]

'WHERE IS POLITICAL SCIENCE GOING' AND WHERE IT SHOULD GO?

What happened? How is it possible that Sartori, who, as the founder of contemporary Italian political science, was influenced and inspired by American political science, never became fully accustomed to his new environment in the United States? We can look for an answer in his exceptional skepticism expressed in a question and answer in one of his later texts:

> Where is political science going? . . . American-type political science . . . is going nowhere. (Sartori 2004d, 786)[12]

What did he have in mind? Although Sartori (1997a, 96) claimed allegiance to an empirical conception of political science, he never affiliated himself with behaviouralism. Rather, in not doing so, he had to reject the 'second scientific revolution' (the first 'revolution' was behaviouralist); that is, the effort 'to make the field more scientific' in the sense of an 'outgrowth of the methodological aspirations of behavioralists and the maturation of political methodology, centred on the use of quantitative, statistical methods of empirical testing' (Munck 2007, 52).[13] Political science (comparative politics) wanted (and still wants) to be, in short, a 'scientifically-orientated' field (Blondel 1997, 117), an objective field founded on hard data. It wants to resemble the natural sciences[14] (Linz 2007, 205), while other approaches are rejected as 'unscientific'. The results of quantitative research are objective and indisputable. They are also comfortable, for there is no need to formulate arguments, theories, concepts and ideas. In short, there is nothing to argue about, with only one exception: methods of measuring. The scientific effort thus shifts from the analysis of a problem to the creation and analysis of methods of data analysis (Huntington 2007, 232). Research, then, is not 'problem-driven' but rather 'technique-driven' (Stepan 2007, 454–55). The result of all this is excessive specialisation, and mainly the sterilisation of political science (comparative politics), which becomes entirely disconnected from reality.

Sartori's empiricism and the scientific nature of his work were entirely different. Political research should be contextual; that is, it should not avoid historical, cultural, linguistic and other circumstances. It should be usable in practice (see more on this shortly) and focused on solving problems, not giving precedence to questions of methodology and research techniques. The goal of political research should not be gathering data and modelling (or even, perhaps, merely recalculating the data) but rather the creation of concepts and theories through comparative research. Closely connected with this is Sartori's understanding (in contrast with that of the mainstream) of the methodology of science. Sartori wrote a number of key methodological texts.[15] It is very important and, in the context described earlier, typical of Sartori that he was interested in methodology not in the sense of research techniques but in the sense of a way of thinking (Sartori 1997a, 95). What interested him was the correctness of thought and use of language. In one of his key methodological texts, *Concept Misformation in Comparative Politics* from 1970, he wrote the following sentence, which was characteristic of his work and says quite a lot:

> In a very crucial sense, there is no methodology without *logos*, without thinking about thinking. (Sartori 1970b, 1033)

Quantification, 'counting', only comes second: 'Briefly put, "think" before counting; and, also, "use logic" in thinking' (Sartori 2004d, 786). It is necessary to first ask a 'what-is' question, and only afterwards, a 'how-much' question (Mair 2014, 73; Sartori 1975). To put it in other words, quality comes before quantity.

ON CONCEPT FORMATION

Of course, one cannot draw the hasty conclusion from the earlier discussion that Sartori always, under all circumstances, stood against quantitative research in political science (Collier and Gerring 2009b, 6; Pasquino 2009, 169). After all, he used it as well. We find quantitative approaches in probably his best-known work, *Parties and Party Systems* (Sartori 2005a), which, alongside Duverger's pioneering *Les partis politiques* (1951), has become the foundation of all contemporary research of party systems (the book won Sartori the Leon Epstein Outstanding Book Award).[16] A quantitative approach, of course, can be used only under the condition that it is built on solid conceptual foundations: 'concept formation stands prior to quantification'

(Sartori 1970b, 1038). What is foundational, in short, is work with concepts, which Sartori's interpretation described as classical (Collier and Mahon 1993, 845). Sartori, in his optimism, was convinced that a social scientist could establish concepts, terms, definitions, etc. through productive analysis. Concepts must be created and used in a semantically and analytically correct and precise manner. Concepts cannot be separated from language and semantics—from natural language, that is, not a formalised language—because bad language (incorrect semantics) leads to bad thought (Sartori 1975; 1984a).[17]

Correct or, on the contrary, incorrect use of concepts is tightly connected with correct or incorrect comparisons—in the words of Sartori (1991a), 'comparing and miscomparing'. Comparisons are crucial because, among other things, they lead to an inspection (confirmation or refutation) of generalising (theoretic) claims. It is, of course, necessary to compare the comparable and not lapse into the creation of a 'cat-dog' (Sartori 1991a, 247). Cat-dogs come about as the result of a combination of several mistakes: 1) parochialism, 2) misclassification, 3) 'degreeism', and 4) conceptual stretching (Sartori 1991a, 247–49). The first of these is an incorrect application of concepts under local conditions without taking their broader (comparative) sense into consideration. For example, we cannot speak of a 'coalition government in the United States' when we know that coalition governments can only form in parliamentary or semi-presidential regimes and not in presidential ones. Misclassification is rooted in the creation of erroneous classes. It is entirely impossible for the class of 'one-party states' to include 'one-party states' like the United States, Japan, Sweden, Norway, India, Mexico, the Soviet Union, China, the communist countries of Eastern Europe and so on, for in each individual case, the 'one party' in question is entirely different. 'Degreeism' consists of an uncritical attempt to deal with differences in type among phenomena as differences in degree; in other words, to place them along a continuum. In one example, democracy could not be separated from nondemocracy; the result would be that each political system in the world (a continuum) would have some amount of both.

Sartori was particularly worried about the issue of conceptual stretching and devoted considerable attention to it. To stretch a concept is to make it overly general and use it to label anything at all. The problem is that, if we use a given concept without regard to given practical conditions, it will lose its fundamental heuristic value and undergo complete empirical vaporisation (Sartori 1970b, 1043). One frequent example is the concept of mobilisation (Pasquino 2009, 169; Sartori 1970b, 1051; 1991a, 249). If we stretch it inappropriately, then we can use it to describe every activity in society. By doing so, of course, we lose sight of the difference between political mobilisation and participation. To put it simply, political mobilisation is imposed from above, while political participation is voluntary and spontaneous. This distinction, simple at first glance, is crucial because it relates to the distinction between politics of a democratic nature and that of an undemocratic nature.

Sartori also devoted much attention to the concept of pluralism because it can be interpreted so broadly that it can be applied to anything at all. If we—erroneously—understand it as simply multiple occurrences (to be in plural) or any kind of social differentiation, then we can—incorrectly—use it in the context of the Soviet Union or the caste system in India. This, however, is not pluralism in the true sense of the word, which is a political (and fundamentally democratic) value (Sartori 1997d; 2000b). Not taking these factors into account leads to a fatal misunderstanding, and incorrect explanation, of the situation.

The examples presented earlier are downright mistakes. On the other hand, it is true that a natural characteristic of concepts is that they are complex and ambiguous and can thus be understood and explained in different ways. Concepts have a range of meanings depending on the degree of their abstraction. From this supposition, it follows that there is not much sense in asking how many meanings a concept has but rather how abstract it is (Mair 2014, 82). Concepts can be sorted according to their degree of abstraction. Here I am of course referencing Sartori's famous ladder of abstraction (Sartori 1970b). High-level concepts are universal and are marked by maximum extent (extension) and minimum content (intension), while low-level concepts are singular; that is, they have minimum extent and maximum content. This distinction is important in maintaining proper use of concepts. If we want to use one concept in multiple situations, we must move up or down along the ladder of abstraction. Sartori's ladder begins with a minimal or minimalistic definition of a given concept. We define the concept only by its most necessary and appropriate defining features. But which are these? This is very difficult to say. Peter Mair (2014, 85) uses the concept of democracy as a good example. If we say that the defining features are competitive (multiple-party) elections, then we undervalue, for example, the question of adherence to fundamental rights and freedoms and we arrive at Zakaria's illiberal democracies. On the contrary, if we focus on rights and freedoms and do not give proper value to elections, we miss the crucial issue of every democratic process: the right of voters to dismiss their government through elections. If we insist on both variables, we approximate Dahl's (1971) polyarchy. But this would place us quite low on the ladder of abstraction, meaning that we would label as democracies only a few examples in practice. In short, as was stated earlier, concepts must be created and subsequently adhered to. If we define a phenomenon poorly or later needlessly redefine it by any means necessary, we will at most create confusion, ambiguity and overlapping of concepts (Collier and Gerring 2009b, 5). If we take a concept that is applicable at one level of abstraction for a given set of cases and apply it at the same level of abstraction for other cases, the result will be confusion.

APPLICABLE KNOWLEDGE

From the beginning of his academic career, Giovanni Sartori (1952; 1974b; 1979; 1997a; 2004d) repeatedly stated that political science should be an applicable science,[18] even in a sort of futurological sense:

> Political science is the science of observing and predicting the most likely possibilities for future development. It is necessary to know the current political reality. (Sartori 1952, 74)

Political scientists should know how to resolve practical problems of politics. Sartori held to this conviction his entire life, and his comparative studies also contained clear views on which solutions to given problems were the most appropriate or, on the other hand, harmful (Sartori 1968; 1994).

Sartori's effort to pursue an applicable science is most evidently visible in one of his later texts, the already classic *Comparative Constitutional Engineering* (Sartori 1994). The book is one large, active contribution to the discussion on how to improve the functioning of contemporary democratic regimes. Sartori raised a whole series of questions on this topic. Which electoral system is most appropriate? Should we give preference to a parliamentary or presidential (or semi-presidential) regime? Which is better, a unicameral parliament or a bicameral one? And so on. Characteristically, Sartori gave clear answers to these questions accompanied by expert arguments, considering the time and place, and was willing to adopt a sharp polemical tone.[19]

In the book, Sartori rather courageously presented his own proposal for the best functioning (not universally ideal) democratic regime: 'alternating presidentialism'. The regime has two engines: a parliamentary one and a presidential one. After parliamentary and presidential elections, which take place at the same time, the regime functions like a parliamentary one. It is only in the case of failure (the fall of an unstable government) that the parliamentary engine is shut off and the presidential engine is started up for the remainder of the term. The presidential period, though, does not have to take place at all and functions more as a deterrent mechanism for the parliament to rethink its dysfunction (Sartori 1994, 153–60).

Comparative Constitutional Engineering is a purely academic book that is, at the same time, very practical. It is an invaluable read for understanding how modern political regimes work and how to reform them if necessary, as well as for comprehending the endless plans of politicians to reform political and constitutional systems or parts of them (mainly electoral systems) and, above all, the pitfalls that can be hidden beneath them.

'UN POLITOLOGO MILITANTE'

Sartori's conviction that political science should be practically oriented can also be seen in his willingness to venture into academic essays and political journalism. His academic essays are mainly represented in two books: *Homo videns* (Sartori 1997b) and *Pluralismo, multiculturalismo e estranei* (Sartori 2000b). In the first work, Sartori warned against what he saw as the harmful influence television and video exert through information that deforms human thought. In the second work, he warned against the doctrine of multiculturalism and its influence on the possibility for immigrants from other cultures to integrate. The two books deal with entirely different topics, but they do have one thing in common: they are controversial, strongly polemical and very pessimistic.

Similarly polemical is Sartori's extensive Italian-language political journalism, in which he became heavily involved after his return to Italy in the 1990s. It was a period of transition from the Italian First Republic to the Second, accompanied by several far-reaching political and institutional changes. Sartori's temperament did not allow him to stay quiet in a situation like this. He became a sort of Italian analogue of Raymond Aron's (1981) 'le spectateur engagé'. He wrote regular columns for *Corriere della Sera* and other newspapers. His commentary was then published in book form (Sartori 2004a; 2006; 2009). He also became a 'TV star' because he regularly appeared on discussion programs on Italian television. He was such a well-known intellectual in Italy that in 1997 he received an offer from the state to become a senator for life—which he declined because he gave preference to intellectual independence (Massari 2014a). He also nearly became involved in various government boards and committees, but this fell through as well. In this case, the cause was his searing criticism, which had made him many political enemies. Sartori's journalistic texts and statements were so sharply critical towards practically the entire Italian political class that he earned the designation of 'a combative political scientist' (*un politologo militante*) (Passigli 2005).

Sartori participated in political discussions with the aim of influencing politicians in their decisions on how to reform the Italian democratic regime. Of course, as laconically noted by Gianfranco Pasquino (2009, 176), 'to no avail'. Sartori's conviction that it is the responsibility of political scientists to try to influence the direction of politics because they know politics better than politicians turned out to be a mere 'enlightenment illusion' that, according to Stefano Passigli (2005, 219), has been refuted many times throughout history. Still, though, for academics, who wish to become involved, the thesis that 'he who knows more must do more' remains an analogue of 'noblesse oblige' and an ethical imperative. Sartori called in vain for reform of the Italian electoral system and unsuccessfully proposed a change from a parliamentary regime to alternating presidentialism (see earlier). Here we see a sort of indirect analogue to what is known as Duverger's paradox (Elgie 2011, 75), in which international academic renown does not bring political influence (in Duverger's case, as an expert) in one's own country.[20] Thus, if political science should be practical and its test is success in applying its findings in practice, then Sartori himself did not pass this test and evidently could not pass it. What is characteristic for him, though, is that in a whole range of cases, later political developments in Italy showed him to be right. His stubbornness did not allow him to make compromises, which led to his isolation (Massari 2014a), but on the other hand, most of the times things turned out as he said they would all the same.[21]

CONCLUSION

Giovanni Sartori was never just a scientist in any narrow, exact understanding. Rather, he was a scholar.[22] A great scholar. He became a true legend even within his lifetime. Of course, legends do not have it easy and are often viewed with controversy. Similarly, their creative legacy is not always unanimously accepted. Not everyone is able to fully appreciate them. Sartori did not avoid controversy and often went against the mainstream. As a result, he lost some of his battles but also won others. His work is filled with one great paradox: he became the greatest Italian political scientist and, in his time, the most famous political journalist, but he was never able to influence Italian politics and his recommendations were never adopted in Italy. At the same time, though, in the end many of his originally rejected views turned out to be true. He is one of the creators and giants of contemporary political science (comparative politics), although its current dominant trend has entirely distanced itself from him. The direction in which the majority of the field is moving is entirely different from his visions, which makes it all the more paradoxical that the starting point was the same: political science (comparative politics) should be an empirical science. The currently predominant 'data cumulating' empiricism, however, has surpassed all measures Sartori could think of. He became an empirical political scientist in an overly empirical political science. Sartori's body of work, though, remains alive and will continue to be so in the future. His concepts were, are and will be used, for without concepts—and, of course, without *his* concepts—political science could hardly exist. Naturally, Sartori (1997a, 99) was aware of this and ultimately evaluated his academic impact positively:

> So, I cannot complain, and indeed I feel good about my overall balance sheet.

NOTES

1. This chapter is a rewritten version of a piece that was originaly published in Czech in the journal *Acta Politologica* 7(1), 2015.
2. These works exist only in the original Italian. Sartori later stopped working in philosophy, at most tending to selected issues in political philosophy, especially in relation to Croce (Sartori 1966b; 1997c)—all, again, in Italian.
3. See Marek Bankowicz's chapter in this book.
4. On this topic, we can mention in passing that Sartori was a sworn critic of democracy with modifiers (see Bankowicz's chapter in this book), which has nothing in common with true (meaning liberal) democracy (without modifiers). The communist regimes in Eastern Europe after 1948 often referred to themselves as 'people's democracies'.
5. Sergio Panunzio was a leading theorist of fascism and a proponent of political science as the theory of the state and doctrines. Other faculties were started during the era of fascism. The 'fascist' origin of the prewar Italian science of politics was one important reason why Sartori, who never had any inclination whatsoever towards fascism, rejected it.
6. Sartori later founded the *Centro Studi di Politica Comparata* as a 'youth training centre' for beginner political scientists; edited the foundational Italian political science handbook *Antologia di scienza politica* (Sartori 1970a), which characteristically met with great criticism from Italian sociologists, constitutional lawyers and political philosophers (Pasquino 2013a); and founded the journal *Rivista Italiana di Scienza Politica*, of which he was editor in chief until 2004.
7. We can mention in passing that, on this issue, he did not really reach an understanding with Norberto Bobbio, who, of course, otherwise played a significant role in the construction of modern Italian political science.
8. Sartori argued against Mosca extensively, especially his theory of elites—above all in his famous book on democracy (Sartori 1987). It is characteristic of Sartori that he did not particularly acknowledge the Italian classics in the study of politics in his texts and rarely cited them. He only maintained a positive attitude towards Croce, whose liberalism was close to his.
9. In this opinion Sartori met with disagreement from the famous Polish sociologist Jerzy J. Wiatr, from whom Sartori (2005a, 204), in *Parties and Party Systems*, took the label 'hegemonic party'. Otherwise, of course, Wiatr also supported a distinction between the sociology of politics and political sociology. According to him, political sociology is a way of understanding politics and society in their mutual interconnectedness rather than an approach to politics limited to social factors at the expense of, for example, geopolitical, biological or purely political factors. Political sociology understood in this way and the sociology of politics share a definite bond, but they are not identical disciplines. Political sociology is the theoretical foundation for the sociology of politics, which is, however, something broader, encompassing not just general theoretical interpretation but also a number of specific claims (Wiatr 1999, 12–13).
10. Here it is worth mentioning Sartori's recollections of the period in question, which reveal much about his character, as well as his political positions: 'Yes, colleagues often ask me about this, they know that I am a fighter. At that time, I had established several conditions: all lecturers had to fully support me, and I alone was authorized to speak at student assemblies. It was awful work. Nobody wanted to do it. Sometimes I slept right at the faculty. When I learned that students were even making phone calls to China, I had the phones disconnected, and then in the winter I turned their heat off. Then all the revolutionaries disappeared, and the protests were over and done with. After that, at the age of forty, I received a gold medal for the development of education and culture usually given to octogenarians' (Truzzi 2014).
11. In this context, it is worth mentioning Hector Schamis's recollection: 'In his tailored Italian suits, he was always stern and very demanding. In class, he used to address us by our last names, and in small seminars he would go around the table, asking us our views on the issue under discussion. I clearly remember his, "And what do you think, Mr. Schamis?" To get Professor Sartori's approval was not easy' (Skach et al. 2009, 343).
12. Sartori writes of 'American-type' political science, not political science as such, but this is inconsequential. The 'research standards' of contemporary (worldwide) political science

(comparative politics) are essentially 'American' (Munck 2007, 32) and Sartori's statement can to a large extent be generalised.

13. The predominantly quantitative nature of contemporary political science (again in the sense of comparative politics) can be demonstrated quantitatively, as Andreas Schedler and Cas Mudde (2010) did in their analysis of articles published in leading comparative politics journals. Their study showed that comparative politics has seen a marked expansion of the use of quantitative methods, primarily in recent years, and that statistical methods have become the dominant method of analysis. According to Schedler and Mudde (2010, 429), regardless of talk of breaking down borders between quantitative and qualitative approaches, comparative politics is a divided field and leading political science journals almost never publish qualitative work in comparative politics.

14. According to Sartori, political science wants to resemble economics. However, 'economists work with real numbers (monetary quantities) embedded in the behaviour of their economic animals, whereas social scientists work with assigned and often arbitrary numerical values' (Sartori 2004d, 785). Similarly, Arend Lijphart (2007, 264) pointed out the problematic nature of data that he sees as primitive. We should thus focus more on making them better and not worry so much about sophisticated methodological techniques.

15. For a collection of texts in English, see Collier and Gerring (2009a). Several of Sartori's important methodological texts exist only in Italian (see Sartori 1979) or were translated into several other languages (mainly Spanish), but not into English.

16. Another quantitative work is the very well-known text he wrote together with Giacomo Sani (Sani and Sartori 1983).

17. Domenico Fisichella (2005, 16) stated that Sartori fought against 'political science illiteracy'.

18. For more on this topic, see Martin Mejstřík's chapter in this book.

19. Particularly famous are his polemics with Arendt Lijphart. See Miroslav Novák's chapter in this book.

20. Duverger's concept of semi-presidentialism, created based on studying the French Fifth Republic, has never been fully accepted by French political scientists and constitutional lawyers.

21. For more on this topic, see Oreste Massari's chapter in this book.

22. Samuel P. Huntington (2007, 224) put it nicely in one interview when he similarly reasoned, 'Q: Do you think of yourself as a scientist? A: Nope. The word "scientist" implies physical sciences and biological sciences. I consider myself a scholar, not a scientist'.

Chapter Three

The Applicability of Political Science

Sartori's Insight

Martin Mejstřík

In the early postwar years, political science in Italy was rather 'underdeveloped' (Leoni 1960) and 'modest' (Bobbio 1961, 231). Even in the 1960s, Giovanni Sartori was still unsatisfied with the pace of development in this newly independent discipline (Sartori 1967).[1] Development was slowed by declared and ferocious opposition from practitioners of more established disciplines, especially law, political philosophy and history. As Norberto Bobbio observed, scholars from those fields simply did not want colleagues competing for limited professorships at the universities. They also had ideological concerns connected with the deposed fascist regime and its support for the faculties of political sciences (Bobbio 1969, 19–25).[2] Another important obstacle to the development of political science in Italy, noted by Leonardo Morlino, was the absence of a recent, seminal text for the discipline, as *Elementi di scienza politica* by Gaetano Mosca (1953) had been for the previous generation. That arrived with the appearance of *Antologia di scienza politica*, edited by Sartori (1970a), and later with his masterpiece, *Parties and Party Systems: A Framework for Analysis* (1976).

The aim of this chapter is to analyse concisely the formation of Sartori's thoughts about political science and their applicability in the real world of politics. In the first part, I will present the initial problems that political science in Italy had to overcome at the beginning of its postwar existence and the role Giovanni Sartori played in that process. This will help us better understand Sartori's relentless drive for the applicability of his discipline. He was above all a comparative political scientist, promoting the method of comparison with a clear practical purpose—helping to guide practical political decision making. In Sartori's own words:

> If we don't want to consider political science a practical and pragmatic knowledge, I cannot understand anymore what we are looking for: in this case we sacrifice our efforts on the altar of sterility, in pursuit of an inconclusive scientism that seems to be, more than anything else, an idol we have built on a pile of inferiority complexes. (Sartori 1954, 17)

But what exactly is the meaning of applicability in political science? Gianfranco Pasquino repeatedly pointed out that political science deals with the ways society constructs and maintains the acceptable political order that is necessary for society's survival. It can't be purely theoretical (Pasquino 2013a). Because it is also an inexact discipline, political science can't be considered an 'applied science'. On the other hand, it is an 'applicable' science, which offers the possibility of applying acquired knowledge to change the existing political setting. It must submit its hypotheses, theories and generalisations to scrutiny in the harsh light of facts (Pasquino 2013b, 243). I will analyse the applicability of political science in the second part of this chapter, recounting Sartori's famous fight in the 1990s for a two-round electoral system in Italy.

INITIAL PROBLEMS

Sartori's life work was the fight against 'illiteracy' in political science, by emphasising the importance of language and lexicology for overcoming excessive emotion and ideology in research (Fisichella 2005, 17).[3] 'Illiteracy' was the first big obstacle Sartori had to overcome on the way towards applicable political science. He tried to clearly distinguish two different disciplines that often were mixed up and confused: 'political science' and 'politology'.[4] As Bobbio has defined it, political science is a scientific discipline with an empirical methodology that analyses different aspects of political reality with the intent of explaining it to a close circle of people working in the same field (Bobbio 1969). That means that the majority of political scientists should give up on providing explanations for a broad nonacademic audience. Sartori vehemently refused to do so. On the contrary, he refused to close himself up in an 'academic ivory tower'. He used precise, plain language to address the masses and to push applicable aspects of political science into practical politics. His approach should not be confused with 'politology'. According to Leonardo Morlino, 'politology' is mere commentary or glossary on political events, without concrete methodology having the goal of interpreting events to the broadest possible audience (Morlino 1989, 5).

Even nowadays, that is in reality exactly what various journalists and political commentators who consider themselves political scientists are doing—just 'politology'.[5] Martin Bull agrees and divides academics dealing with political science into two categories: 'political scientists', who use theories and methods to analyse political reality, and 'political observers', who comment upon and interpret political events without a methodology (Bull 2015).

The problem was even more visible in Italian politics. Not only commentators mixed up the two disciplines. So did many researchers coming from related social sciences. Joseph LaPalombara attributes this blurring of boundaries to an 'identity crisis' of the original Italian political scientists. Sartori included, they had to operate in an intellectually hostile academic culture in which they had to disguise themselves as professors of sociology, philosophy or history (LaPalombara 1986, 62). This behaviour greatly complicated the establishment of political science as an independent discipline with strong methodology and high-quality publishing outputs. Early political scientists had to mix their own approaches with those of political philosophy, law, history and economy. They opened political science research to scientists and researchers from other fields, regardless of the fact that political science has a different perspective, for which a different methodology and different research techniques are needed (Bobbio 1969, 15).

Bobbio was also the first to define the differences between these disciplines.[6] According to him, lawyers and political scientist are both interested in typologies and abstract concepts. Lawyers deal with behaviours regulated by a given legal system, whereas political scientists study the motivations and the consequences of those behaviours. The main difference between a political scientist and a historian lies in the fact that political scientists are applying a methodology of empirical science to the analysis of general concepts and mass phenomena (following a neopositivist philosophy), while historians deal with individual acts in the past and specific persons, all of them unique and irreducible. As Bobbio laconically summarized,

> While jurists have shown themselves to be unaware of political science, historians know it exists but do not take it into account. (Bobbio 1969, 22)

Sartori himself insisted on a coherent differentiation between philosophy and history. He proposed concrete steps in political practice (thus making political science 'applicable'). He created a special language and his famous 'concept formatting' (Sartori 1970b). He saw philosophy as 'hard to understand' and political science as 'hard to do' (Sartori 1959, 64).

Hard, however, does not mean impossible. There are approaches and rules which allow the gathering of empirical evidence of political reality. It was Sartori who compiled those rules based on Bobbio's view of political philosophy (Bobbio 1969). Expanding on Bobbio's work, Sartori extrapolated a series of steps for making the concepts of political science applicable to the real world: 1) empirical verification; 2) descriptive explanation; 3) abandonment of value judgements;[7] 4) combinability; and 5) operationality and operativity (Sartori 1979, 220).

Sartori recognised three main differences between political science and philosophy: political science uses variables; it has a defined language describing empirical observations; and it is applicable, thus defining a relationship between means and goals (Sola 2005, 47). Regarding the last point, political science has to use empirical research as a tool for both creating and confirming a theory to demonstrate that it is operative and applicable in political practice.

According to Stefano Passigli, political science as an 'applied science' does not, however, clarify whether scientific discourse can find the means to an end. Defining that means leaves behind the realm of scientific discourse and enters the field of value choices. On the other hand, political science cannot be limited only to seeking an objective means to an end. It must also verify the congruity of these ends with respect to universally valid values (Passigli 2005, 219). Sartori's position in this debate was firmly on the side of full autonomy for political science, which should not only analyse events but also apply values and scientific knowledge, in contrast to the axiological discourse of political philosophy (Sartori 1991b).

Sartori did not reject history as a discipline per se, but he warned against following the same conceptual and methodological approach as historians do. At the same time, he stressed the necessity of maintaining strict, well-defined methods, regardless of whether the phenomenon being analysed is in the past or the present or will happen in the future (LaPalombara 1986, 63). In other words, political science should not be retrospective and must deal with the present in order to influence the course of events in the future (Sartori 1952, 61).

Sartori was also very cautious about permitting sociology to have too much influence on the methodology and theories of political science. He criticised other political scientists for the excessive use of 'sociological reductionism', leading them to operate only with dependent variables and reach a state in which politicians do not cause anything but only depend on others (Sartori 1968a). It goes without saying that that would make the applicability of political science impossible. As LaPalombara stated, even if there are some benefits of using the sociological approach in political science, the costs far exceed the advantages (LaPalombara 1973).

In order to construct political science as a practical, applicable discipline, Sartori believed it is necessary to base it on observation and to make predictions of the most likely options for the future development of a political system. To do so, he considered it highly important to know political reality thoroughly. However, this is something of which historians are incapable; as a result, they suffer from 'fear of the future' (Sartori 1952, 74). Sartori's understanding of politics reflects this view. He saw political science as an autonomous, specialised science that can be approached from two directions: 1) a symbolic approach that takes into consideration the interpretations, beliefs, ideals and knowledge that underlie and guide political action;[8] and 2) an institutional approach that further distinguishes between descriptive and prescriptive approaches to political reality (Sola 2005, 50).[9] Sartori drew the conclusion that political science must make the language of practical politics its main focus and then ask to what extent ideology conditions the attitudes, choices and behaviour of political actors. He added a caveat that 'research about politics can't be conducted using the same language in which politics is "done"' (Sartori 1959, 65).

CONSTITUTIONAL ENGINEERING

The area in which Sartori considered the applicability of political science to be most important was in what he called 'constitutional engineering'. Even before he wrote his famous book *Comparative Constitutional Engineering*, Sartori became an ardent advocate of liberal democracy because he believed that 'liberalism is the only engineering in history where the goal is really achieved by its means . . . it's a project that works' (Sartori 1987, 386). Sartori also pointed out that the biggest advantage of the link between modern democracy and liberalism is the fact that

> we are not free because we want the laws adopted by our own representatives. We are free because we limit and control their power to enact them. (Sartori 1987, 321)

This citation from *The Theory of Democracy Revisited* is a clear example of Sartori's dedication to defending liberalism against the tyranny of both segments of society, those who are in control and those who are controlled. That is why he gradually developed his idea of constitutional engineering, which he viewed as the main tool for protecting the freedom of the individual from unlimited state power. The best way he knew to apply constitutional engineering in political practice was to carve out and influence political parties, which usually exist outside the constitutional framework but can be affected by very simple mechanisms, such as a change in electoral law. Sartori believed that the main leverage available to influence and defend liberal democracy lies in the composition of the party system itself and in the 'manipulation' of the political parties within it. No wonder Sartori saw the role of political parties in postwar European party systems to be critical.

Sartori did not hesitate to criticise colleagues, especially Stein Rokkan and Maurice Duverger, who didn't believe in the importance of the applicability of political science or who downplayed the influence of electoral systems on party systems (Sartori 1976, 291). Sartori later explained how electoral systems could be designed, in the presence of two different party systems. Table 3.1 shows the four variables he recognised and the effect they can have on political outcomes (Sartori 1982, 118).

As Pasquino interpreted table 3.1, he supported Sartori's approach and stressed the effect that electoral systems can have not only on individual parties but also on whole party systems as well (Pasquino 2005, 204). This is a clear example of the application of political science to polity building, constructing a political system based on the combined effects of electoral law and party system. Done incorrectly, with no regard to predictable results, it could end up like the *Mattarellum*, a mixed electoral system introduced in Italy at the beginning of the so-called Second Republic. Pasquino wrote,

> Application of an electoral system that is not strong enough, like the *Mattarellum*, to a relatively weak party system, as was the Italian one in 1994, caught up as it was in a complex, differentiated process of deconstruction and reconsolidation, would not have been able to produce significant and durable effects automatically. (Pasquino 2005, 205)

It is no surprise that Sartori became an ardent critique of the *Mattarellum* for its entire eleven years of existence.[10]

Sartori also warned of the dangers of applying constitutional engineering beyond parties and party systems. That occurs when there are changes in constitutional order or executive power without corresponding reform of electoral laws and party systems. Sartori praised the Fifth French Republic as a well-done transformation. He considered attempts to apply the same semi-presidential model in Latin America, with its atomized party systems, to be a nonfunctional failure (Sartori 1976, 16). He also feared any shift in the hegemony of power 'from the rule of law to rule by law' (Sartori 1987, 327).[11] In other words, he began to worry when judicial power started to play a political-legislative role instead of its usual role of interpreting laws. That happened at the end of the so-called First Italian Republic in 1992 with the *Mani*

Table 3.1.

Party system	Electoral system		
		Strong (majoritarian)	*Weak* (proportional)
	Strong (structured)	Reductive effect (United Kingdom)	Counterbalancing effect (Austria, Spain)
	Weak (nonstructured)	Blocking effect (India)	No effect

Source: Pasquino 2005, 204.

pulite. The judiciary involved itself wholesale in the turbulent political events Sartori witnessed and criticised as a columnist writing for the most important Italian newspaper, *Corriere della Sera*. Sartori's articles were subsequently republished in a book called *Seconda Repubblica? Sì, ma bene* (Sartori 1992).

COMMITTED POLITICAL SCIENCE

The relationship between the 'ivory tower' world of academia and practical politics has always been contentious. Active engagement in political life has been considered by some to be a necessity or even an obligation. On the other hand, the vast majority of intellectuals have seen it as 'treason' to the proper role of science (see Benda 1976). In the Italian context, a similar 'fight' took place in the first half of the twentieth century between the right-wing interventionism of Gabriele D'Annunzio and the organic left-wing intellectualism of Antonio Gramsci on one side and the detachment of Giuseppe Prezzolini and the isolationism of the hermetic poets[12] on the other (Passigli 2005, 214). Isolationism lost the struggle with the fall of fascism. In the first postwar years, the political culture of Italy was dominated by the idealism of Benedetto Croce, by Marxist radical historical determinism and by the anti-Enlightenment attitude of the Catholic Church.

The most influential groups of public intellectuals were most heavily influenced by the thoughts and ideas of Karl Marx. This was also the case in the university communities; students and professors were influenced by scientific approaches which were highly deterministic and hostile to theoretical formulations that did not conform to the Marxist vision of the world. Marxism shared the same view as modern sociology (see earlier) that institutions and political phenomena are dependent on economic and social factors in a society (LaPalombara 1986, 69). No wonder then that these approaches were not exactly friendly to the establishment of a new, empirically based discipline. The situation of the newly (re)born Italian political science was quite difficult. The traditions of the other academic disciplines, the structure of power in the university and the intellectual environment in the country tended to keep political science bound to anti-empirical, or at least nonempirical, research (Leoni 1960).

As practitioners of a not yet fully established discipline, Italian political scientists tended to hew to idealist traditions and not actively participate in political events. Political scientists feared that their too active involvement in public affairs would undermine the respect for their discipline that they were diligently trying to forge.[13] As Passigli recalled, even Sartori himself was not involved in public activities at the beginning of his career. He was more interested in political philosophy, the theory of democracy and later the methodology of social science (Passigli 2005, 215). Only with the earlier mentioned constitutional engineering did Sartori turn to a vision of applied political science. After studying the various factors that influence political events, he came to the conclusion that only institutions can be modified in the short term. He therefore started to explore the possibility of the 'applied engineering' of party and electoral systems.

Although Sartori pioneered applied political science in Italy, on the world stage he took ideas from David Easton, who had already explicitly promoted the applicability of political science in his 1953 book *The Political System: An Inquiry into the State of Political Science*.[14] In Sartori's case, the first trace of his call for making political science an applicable discipline can be found in his 1970 chapter of *Antologia di scienza politica* (Sartori 1970a) and in his article 'La politica come scienza', published in 1972 in the *Rivista Italiana di Scienza Politica* (Sartori 1972). There he expressed his belief in the possibility and utility of applied political science. His belief was not yet based on his own political activism but rather on his firm conviction that those who possess knowledge of political science have to use it to influence the course of political events. This led him to the clear conclusion that the one who knows more has to do more, in other words, is bound by an ethical imperative (Passigli 2005, 219).

During the 1980s, Sartori increasingly focused on an empirical and applicable kind of political science that is not based on value choices and does not aspire to an absolute imperative but instead explains the political reality and influences the behaviour of political actors based on the correlation 'if . . . then . . .'. For example, if we have a fragmented party system and our objective is effective government through the reduction of party fragmentation, the only efficient instrument in the short run would be modification of the electoral system and not revision of the entire constitution and form of government (Passigli 2005, 225).

Not all political scientists in Italy, however, took the same approach to the applicability of political science as Sartori. Some of them argued that it is society itself which can change political behaviour rather than political scientists and their propositions (see Panebianco 1989). Another group of academics considered politics almost as a mathematical game, emphasising quantification and measuring relevance, which leads to examining only that which is measurable. The consequence of this approach is the loss of normativity and theory in politics (Regalia and Valbruzzi 2013, 27–29). Those quantitative scientists are limited to drawing conclusions that are mostly already written in their premises and often even in their hypotheses (Pasquino 2013b, 244).

PRACTICAL TEST

Giovanni Sartori came back to Italy from the United States in 1992 and immediately started to engage in the debate over the transformation of the so-called First Italian Republic. The majority of 'political observers' and even political scientists were unprepared for the collapse of the First Republic and for the necessary transformation of the party system. This was because they refused to follow Sartorian rules of comparative research and too often applied the term 'anomaly' to political events, institutions and even parties. If too many cases are considered anomalous, there is no place for their explanation, categorisation and generalisation. Following up his previous theoretical work on applicability, Sartori soon understood that the new electoral law would be the crucial part of the whole transformation. According to his previous theories, a good electoral system must not only convert votes into parliamentary seats without excessive distortion but must also allow formation of a stable and effective government. In other words, electoral systems must not only provide for representation of voters but also determine how a government is formed.

It is easy to understand from Sartori's definition of the ideal electoral system that he became a harsh critic of the *Mattarellum*. He saw its main defect in its allocation of 75 percent of the seats in Parliament to single-member districts, filled by the first-past-the-post voting method. Sartori warned that in a party system characterised by excessive party fragmentation, even a small, marginal party can play a decisive role by bringing to a potential coalition the votes necessary to make it successful (Sartori 1995b, 39–41). The *Mattarellum* would give these small political entities 'blackmail potential'[15] and allow them to play a much more important role in the party system than they deserved.[16] The result was electoral coalitions that were unable to construct strong and united governments. This sacrifice of governing ability on the altar of stability was heavily criticised by Sartori. He emphasised that a government can be stable but inefficient. It would not make any real contribution to effective governing, which depends on a homogeneous coalition, especially in a party system characterised by a large number of 'relevant' parties, as in Italy after 1994 (Passigli 2005, 224). This homogeneity, however, can be achieved only if party fragmentation is gradually reduced, which requires instruments that are capable of doing that, for example, Sartori's constitutional engineering and concomitant changes in the electoral law (see Sartori 1976; 1984b).

Sartori has quite clear suggestions for best improving the governability and effectivity of the Italian party system. He proposed an 'alternating presidentialism' together with a two-round electoral system in single-member constituencies inspired by the French Fifth Republic (Sartori 1992). In his own words:

> Almost all now agree that we must promptly launch a majority-type electoral reform. But there are many majority-type solutions, and to say 'majoritarian', without specifying, helps to make confusion. The proper majoritarian electoral systems are basically two: 'dry' uninominal (one-round) and uninominal two-round. . . . With 'dry' uninominal, it often happens that the winner is elected by a relative majority, resulting in roaring distortions. . . . The case is completely different with the two-round system. In the first round, voters can freely express their first preference; but they will be induced to concentrate their votes after seeing the results of the first round, making them converge on the possible winners. Technically, the merit of a two-round system is that the winner cannot be from the 'greater minority'. Psychologically, the advantage of the two-round system is that the voter who is induced to change his vote does not feel forced by the electoral system but, if anything, by the vote of others. (Sartori 1995b, 15–17)

This is an example of how Sartori tried to influence public opinion. It was published in *Corriere della Sera* on 12 October 1992, and used simple, precise language to apply his well-structured concepts to the political reality of a collapsing party system. As Oreste Massari describes in the following chapter, Sartori actively 'lobbied' for his proposition of a new electoral system. In the same way, Sartori openly criticised not only the *Mattarellum* but also the idea of a 'strong premiership' and even the direct election of the head of government. Sartori pointed out that the *Mattarellum*'s type of electoral system had not been put to the test anywhere else and that it could bring about a strongly negative element of rigidity and incorrigibility. He also noticed that even a powerful, immovable prime minister could not solve the problem of governability—he will be efficient only when he has a majority in Parliament, otherwise he will end up a lonely general, without the support of even his own troops (Sartori 1995b, 42–45).

Sartori tried to assert his views on a new party system in his home country, but he failed spectacularly. However, that does not mean that political science is not applicable. Massari's chapter of this book explains more thoroughly why Sartori could not succeed.

CONCLUSION

Giovanni Sartori fought a hard fight in the name of the applicability of political science. Initially, he had to overcome many obstacles arising from the underdeveloped status of political science in postwar Italy. As the first, and for many years the only, professor of political science in the country, he had to cope with colleagues from other disciplines who had different views on methodology and scientific knowledge. That only strengthened his determination to construct a fully independent discipline with an empirical methodology and precise language. It was not far from that to 'constitutional engineering' and his attempts to apply individual concepts to political reality.

When Sartori returned from the United States, he found an ideal laboratory for applying his theories. Several things favoured his recommendations. It was an appropriate time, during the transformation between two party systems; there was a strong force of public opinion behind institutional reforms; and the political class was willing to cooperate with academic experts. It was probably simple human stubbornness and unwillingness to compromise that thwarted his success (Massari 2014a). However, we should not dismiss the applicability of political science as a whole for that reason.

I conclude with a paraphrase from none other than Raymond Aron, who said that if the political scientist

> pretends to act as a man of science or formulate only scientific comments he would be less scientifically honest. (Aron 1960b, 123)

Giovanni Sartori did not succeed in his endeavour to apply his recommendations in political practice, but throughout his whole academic life he demonstrated his scientific honesty.

NOTES

1. As proof of the unsatisfactory conditions of Italian political science in the 1950s, we can point to the fate of the first two political science journals in Italy. In the quarterly *Il Politico*, only 10 percent of its articles could be considered to be 'political science'. The journal *Studi politici* had interrupted its triannual publication for two years before it was finally shut down in 1961 (Morlino 1989, 10).

2. For more about pre-Sartorian political science in Italy, see Michal Kubát's chapter in this book.

3. The basic principle of political science thus should be the principle of exploring reality with empirical research and without excessive emotion.

4. A comparison to astronomy and astrology could be used as a very loose metaphor.

5. Putting too much emphasis on the anomaly of Italy in various sectors has become the biggest obstacle to the development of political science in Italy today, together with its low internationalisation and virtually nonexistent studies of other countries.

6. Originally, the first person who tried to define political science in postwar Italy was Bruno Leoni in 1949. He viewed political science as an empirical discipline in the Weberian style that had to fight against the formalism of lawyers and the unpreparedness of the political class (Sola 2005, 44–45). Sartori later became an ardent advocate of Leoni's appeal to test political science against the realities of the political system.

7. In the Italian original Sartori used the term *avalutatività*, which was introduced to the social sciences by Max Weber. In general, *avalutatività* means the refusal to interject value judgements into a historical-social investigation. The scholar conducting research must reveal the values that inspire social choices, but he should not assume them him- or herself as criteria for making judgements. Weber explained how values can affect the results of a social science investigation in his 1904 essay *The Objectivity of Knowledge in Social Science and Social Policy* (Whimster 2003, 359–406).

8. Within the symbolic approach to politics, Sartori further distinguished two different approaches: denotation (extending concepts to the totality of objects) and connotation (connect-

ing characteristics contained within the concepts) (Sartori 1979, 277). There is an inverse relationship between these two approaches. Higher denotation of a concept (that is, it is more generalised) is accompanied by lower connotation (it is less specific, with fewer common attributes). For more detail, see the description of Sartori's 'ladder of abstraction' in Michal Kubát's chapter of this book.

9. The descriptive approach is about institutional structures and procedures. On the other hand, the prescriptive approach deals with values, expectations and ideals. Usually all studies of political phenomena entail a combination of both (Sola 1989).

10. He was the first to use this label for the electoral system in his 9 June 1993 column in *Corriere della Sera*. For more detail about Sartori's struggle with electoral systems in Italy, see Oreste Massari's chapter in this book.

11. Sartori repeatedly criticised the rigid separation of powers and the low degree of autonomy of the judiciary in postwar European constitutions. On the other hand, he praised the US Constitution for its clean and simple liberalism and co-equal position for judicial power. Current political developments in the United States confirm his high opinion of its constitution. Even an unconventional president such as Donald Trump is subject to the checks and balances it establishes. The fate of his Executive Order 13769 (the so-called Muslim ban) revoked in February 2017 at the hands of a single federal judge serves as an illustrative example.

12. *Ermetismo* was an obscure and difficult style of Italian poetry in the 1930s. It was inspired by French decadents and expounded a mystical conception of poetry, promoting hidden, 'hermetic' characters and presenting a sequence of analogies that were difficult to interpret. The isolationism and rejection of any social and political involvement by *Ermetismo*'s authors was motivated by their wish to totally detach from fascist culture. The leading figure among them, Salvatore Quasimodo, won the Nobel Prize in Literature in 1959.

13. On the other hand, leading figures from more established fields, such as history and law, played a visible role in the postwar political events, *in primis* among them historian Benedetto Croce and jurist Enrico De Nicola. Their activism culminated in the highly polarised 1970s and blocked space for objective empirical science (Bull 2015, 188).

14. Sartori considered Easton too quantitative and his theories too abstract. He found Easton's earlier mentioned book to be of inferior quality (Sartori 1986, 109). On the other hand, Sartori praised two other American quantitative political scientists who had a significant impact on his 'practical' perception of the discipline: Carl Friedrich and his *Constitutional Government and Democracy* (Friedrich 1950) and Gabriel Almond with his book *The Politics of the Developing Areas* (Almond and Coleman 1960).

15. The concept of the 'blackmail potential' was introduced for the first time by none other than Sartori, even though he was inspired by the notion of the blackmail party of Anthony Downs (Sartori 1976, 123).

16. As the most blatant example we can mention the case of the Union of Democrats for Europe (UDEUR) led by Clemente Mastella. This Christian Democratic Centre party had been founded in 1999 by splinter groups of the former Christian Democracy, and it had its moments of glory in the Italian general election in 2006 when the party obtained 1.4 percent of the votes having elected ten deputies and three senators. When Mastella, then Minister of Justice in Prodi's government, resigned due to ongoing investigation of his person, he decided to bring down with him the whole multicoalition government composed of thirteen parties and backed by another ten in Parliament.

Chapter Four

Giovanni Sartori and the Democracy of the Italian Second Republic[1]

Oreste Massari

Giovanni Sartori is recognised as one of the most important theorists of democracy, to such an extent that he can be now considered a 'classic' thinker in the field. His first book on the subject, *Democrazia e definizioni*, was published in 1957, and his last, *La democrazia in trenta lezioni*, was released in 2008. In between, he produced two volumes of his *Theory of Democracy Revisited* in 1987. Democracy is today studied both in relation to democratic theory, that is, the theory of representative democracy, and in relation to liberal constitutionalism. Sartori's contribution, however, is not limited to the theoretical dimension (such as his studies of political theory, which were essential preliminary steps on the way to his eventual perspective on political reality). Sartori contributed over time with analyses of the institutions, actors and processes of democracy itself, including political representatives, parliaments, party systems and parties (*Parties and Party Systems* is a seminal work of his from 1976), as well as electoral systems, comparative constitutional engineering, etc.

Sartori not only discussed the theory of democracy but also analysed its institutions and actors; he was interested not only in the elements of political science but also in its theoretic categories. On a broader level, this close connection between theory and empirical analysis, between theory and practice (engineering), between concepts and empirical data and between qualitative research and quantitative research characterised all of Sartori's work. It influences the logical construction of his research methodology, especially in the field of comparative politics (his 'singular comparative method'). This connection can also be found in earlier classic works of political science, but regrettably it has been lost as a result of the ever-increasing fragmentation of research, the drastic reduction in the conceptual and theoretic dimensions and simultaneously the increasingly dominant use of quantitative and statistical techniques.

When Sartori sets about examining Italian democracy and its political-institutional system, he is particularly qualified to do so, both on the theoretical level and in terms of what Sartori defines as 'comparative constitutional engineering'. It should be recalled, however, that Italian democracy underwent two distinct phases over the course of its republican history, commonly referred to in the press as the First and the Second Republics. The first phase spanned from 1948 (when a new constitution was approved) to 1992–1994 and the collapse of the traditional party system, which, for better or worse, had sustained the life of the Republic until then. The second phase dates from 1994 to the present and is characterised by an attempt to create a majoritarian democracy in Italy.

THE FIRST PHASE OF ITALIAN DEMOCRACY: 1948–1992

For Sartori, the fundamental problem associated with the first phase of Italian democracy lay not so much in its institutional structure as in its party system, as has been widely recognised. Italy is a case study in 'polarised pluralism' and is thus a 'difficult democracy'. As everywhere else such a democracy has existed (the Weimar Republic, the Spanish Republic 1931–1939, the French Fourth Republic and Chile), it was inevitably bound to collapse or fail. Constitutional and institutional problems (the electoral system, the form of government, etc.) are secondary in importance to those arising from an extreme, multipolar party system and from parties that themselves are highly dysfunctional actors in the parliamentary regime.

Nevertheless, Sartori had high regard for political parties, and he deemed them to be structures that are complex, necessary and fundamental to democracy (Massari 2014b). It could even be said that he considered parties to be noble, both in terms of their origin and of their contributions to the correct functioning of democracy. However, they can malfunction and present a threat to democracy. This problem is not particularly linked to their degree of internal democracy. Sartori was consistently lukewarm if not entirely skeptical about the value of intraparty primaries. The competitive view of democracy shared by both Sartori and Schumpeter doesn't require parties to be internally democratic but merely united and cohesive. In *Ingegneria costituzionale comparata*, Sartori (1995b) introduced the concept of 'parliamentary-fit parties', or parties that are suitable for the task of making a parliamentary form of government work. The example of the British Parliament shows that parties must be even more disciplined and cohesive than under a presidential system. In the Italian First Republic, however, we had antisystem parties (the Italian Social Movement [MSI] and the Italian Communist Party [PCI]), which represented two extreme poles of the left-right 'continuum'. Given the intensity of the ideological distance that separated them, the direction of political and electoral competition was centrifugal and made alternation of governments impossible. Certainly, even the pro-system parties—ruling parties such as the Christian Democrats (DC)—are not exempt from problems. Their main defect is their tolerance for self-interested groups, which for Sartori results in outright factionalism. In various essays written on Italian parties as early as the 1970s and 1980s, Sartori advocated 'electoral engineering' as a corrective. He contended that the proportional system does not in itself cause the number of parties to multiply, but it nevertheless multiplies the number of factions and favours ideological divisions (Massari 2014b). It is clear, however, that during the early period of the First Republic, advocating electoral reform that abolished proportional representation was of limited importance compared to the significance it would later take on when the First Republic began to disintegrate and self-destruct in the late 1980s. Pasquino considers this disintegration and self-destruction of the system to be dominated by the parties (Pasquino 1982).

During the First Republic, Sartori featured strongly as one of the leading protagonists in the intense debates about the anti-system nature of the PCI, even when that party was evolving towards a more pro-Western stance. The PCI's pro-Western positions called into serious question the assumptions of the theory of polarised pluralism, at least as it applied to Italy in the 1970s and 1980s. Answering his critics, Sartori himself admitted that 'the painful and irritating point is the PCI' (Sartori 1982, 299). That point was the leading source of disagreement between Sartori and many political scientists, both Italian and foreign, including many of the Florentine academic's own students (one need only think of Leonardi, Putnam, Tarrow, Farneti, Pasquino, Graziano and Passigli). The crux of their disagreement was the anti-system nature of the PCI and its transformation. This was not purely theoretical or interpretative, from an analytical perspective. It was implicitly and inevitably practical politics. Berlinguer's PCI was distancing itself from Moscow, launching Eurocommunism, proposing a historic compromise, was increasingly portraying itself as a responsible and stabilising force during a time of terrorism and the Moro affair and was garnering increasing support both internally and internationally. At that time, whether he liked it or not, Sartori personified the indefatigable standard-bearer for anticommunism (anticommunist but liberal). In the Italy of the First Republic and in progressive intellectual circles, this constituted a sort of black mark of shame, and whoever so marked themselves was automatically associated with the right. In Italy, 'the right' did not have a good reputation. It is in this context that the legend was born that Sartori abandoned Italy for America in 1976 to protest the PCI's advance in Italy. It is important to remember these events in order to better understand Sartori's later role in the Second Republic.

As we have seen, Sartori was a strong critic of the Italian parties of the so-called First Republic and in particular of the PCI. However, this was nothing in comparison to the uneasiness and dismay that he must have felt in the face of new parties and certain new leaders, whom he incessantly denounced over twenty years in editorials he wrote for *Corriere della Sera*. For Sartori, as a democracy theorist and a scholar of parties and party systems, it wasn't easy to see one of the largest ruling parties in the hands of a TV broadcasting mogul whose governmental and business positions presented a clear conflict of interests (Passigli 2001). Nor was it easy to see the return of a regional party that was sometimes anti-system; to see the proliferation of personalized and, in various ways, populist parties; to see the dissolution of many structures for channelling and expressing political impulses; to see the dominance of factions within parties; and finally to see the success of a movement that imposed a binding mandate upon its parliamentarians, which in his view violated Art. 67 of the Italian Constitution. It is peculiar that the least objectionable party, relatively speaking, was the Democratic Party (PD), the party that evolved from the PCI (and also from the DC), which as we shall see carried on more than one sometimes intensive dialogue on institutional reforms.

THE FIRST YEARS OF THE SECOND REPUBLIC

Although its democratic regime did not collapse, Italy witnessed the failure of its traditional party system between 1992 and 1994 and the beginning of a long and as yet unfinished transition period. It is during this period that problems related to constitutional, institutional and electoral system reform burst onto the political scene, problems that Matteo Renzi's Italy was still struggling to resolve in 2016. One need only recall that there were three bicameral commissions in succession to study constitutional reform (Bozzi 1983–1985, Iotti-De Mita 1992–1994 and D'Alema 1997–1998). Many expert committees on constitutional reform have been nominated by the head of state or by the government. At least eight electoral referenda were held, some of which achieved a quorum of voters and some of which did not. Since the beginning of this period we have seen four different electoral systems, with yet a fifth system being the object of discussion in recent months.

The most significant problem Italy was facing in the 1990s was clear in the minds of public opinion and those of its political, economic and intellectual establishment: constitutional reform, including changing the form of government, the laws regulating justice, the election law and the form of the state itself. It was natural that a person such as Sartori would become the leading authority in the field. It so happened that precisely during this period, in 1994, Sartori returned permanently to Italy, although he would continue to travel back and forth to New York from time to time. His return not only signified the arrival of a great intellectual but also was seen as the reappearance of an individual who could play a decisive role in political affairs. After all, at the beginning of the 1990s Sartori had intensified his writing as a columnist for the most influential and widely read Italian daily newspaper, the *Corriere della Sera*. His editorials were often caustic and piercing, in the personalized style so typical of the Florentine and Tuscan tradition. They were highly influential and were as eagerly anticipated as they were feared. Sartori's editorials would eventually be gathered together in two volumes (Sartori 2004a; 2006). In the early 1990s, Sartori published various books, which were specifically dedicated to political reform in Italy: *Seconda Repubblica? Sì, ma bene* (Sartori 1992); *Democrazia: cosa è* (Sartori 1993); *Come sbagliare le riforme* (Sartori 1995a). In particular, 1994 saw the release of his book in English, *Comparative Constitutional Engineering* (Sartori 1994), which was probably the most successful and systematic work on the subject. It was translated into many languages, including Italian in 1995 (Sartori 1995b). The various Italian editions, six as of 2017, also contained brief essays in their appendices, each offering an update on the state of the political arts.

During that period, then, the popularity of the Florentine scholar was soaring. Sartori became a television star, receiving invitations from all the main talk shows. His legitimacy as an expert on constitutional reform was beyond question and universally accepted, not least due to his high international profile and the recognition he had earned in the United States and worldwide. It is no coincidence that this period saw him receiving many honours and national awards: *Honoris Causa* degrees from the Accademia dei Lincei and the University of Genova in 1992 and the Award for Social Sciences by the Italian prime minister in 1994. The consensus regarding his stature spread across the political spectrum; he was respected both on the right and the left. This consensus, and Satori's legitimacy as a scholar of politics, was further reinforced by the fact that during the 1990s many political scientists who had once been his students became directly involved in politics, both on the right and on the left of the political divide. They served not only as parliamentarians but also as members of various bicameral commissions for reform, and even as government ministers: for example, Gianfranco Pasquino, Stefano Passigli, Domenico Fisichella and Giuliano Urbani. These individuals, all of whom were influential in various ways on the political and intellectual scene, treated Sartori with the utmost deference and respect, given that they considered him a sort of *nume tutelare*. Incidentally, it should be noted that it was precisely during the 1990s that Italian political science, of which Sartori was recognised as the progenitor, enjoyed its greatest degree of influence and visibility.

The enormous respect Sartori enjoyed throughout and beyond the Italian political establishment can be confirmed by recalling certain episodes, some of which are well known and others of which are not.

First, it should be recalled that Sartori was expected to serve as Minister for Constitutional Reform in the grand coalition government attempted by Antonio Maccanico in 1996. Maccanico's attempt to put together a reform-minded government in the first months of 1996 followed the collapse of Berlusconi's first government and the breakdown of Lamberto Dini's caretaker government. It was based on a commitment to introduce a two-round electoral system in Italy, similar to the French model, and a semi-presidential form of government, adapted to the Italian parliamentary tradition. This was clearly a programme that fully reflected Sartori's ideas on the subject. As early as 1991, first in his column in the *Corriere della Sera* and subsequently in his short volume *Seconda Repubblica? Sì, ma bene* in 1992, Sartori (1992) proposed an 'alternating presidentialism' as the most desirable outcome of the Italian political transition.

Maccanico's attempt to form a government failed after only a few days, not least due to a decision by the National Alliance leader, Gianfranco Fini, to support calling a snap election, which he mistakenly thought he could win. Fini subsequently admitted publicly that he regretted his decision. Maccanico's lack of success was also due to the hostility that Romano Prodi and Pier Ferdinando Casini felt for the reform project, to Berlusconi's U-turn to supporting Fini and perhaps also to a rebuke by the then president of the Republic, Oscar Luigi Scalfaro, addressed to those who sought to copy foreign solutions rather than seek a purely Italian way forward.

It should be noted that the only window of opportunity for the adoption of a kind of semi-presidentialism in Italy opened between 1996 and 1998, only to close again once and for all. The first two Bicameral Commissions did not consider the semi-presidential option. The idea resurfaced in 1996–1998, initially as Maccanico attempted to form a government, and then in D'Alema's Bicameral Commission in 1997–1998.

The D'Alema Commission approved the semi-presidential option, presented in opposition to the so-called strong premiership, at its session on 4 June 1997 thanks to a sudden and suspiciously favourable vote by the Northern League (LN), which up to that point had not participated in the work of the Commission. It passed with thirty-six votes in favour, including the six votes from the LN, against thirty-one votes for the strong premiership option.

A particularly 'moderate' form of semi-presidentialism was chosen, giving the president very few powers, which were even further diluted as several amendments were approved. What tipped the balance against semi-presidentialism, however, was that this accord was not built upon a common agreement of major political parties, but rather it was agreed at the famous dinner at Gianni Letta's house which took place on 18 June 1997 and was attended by Franco Marini, Gianfranco Fini, Silvio Berlusconi, Massimo D'Alema and Cesare Salvi. The result was the famous 'Pie Agreement' (*Patto della crostata*) proposing that there would be a guarantor president and a two-round electoral system for Parliament. The parties' candidates for premier would be made clear to voters within this electoral model.

It should be noted that all of the smaller parties also agreed with this scheme (the Italian People's Party, the Communist Refoundation Party and the Federation of the Greens). What was going on? Once a 'moderate' form of semi-presidentialism had been approved, the major parties immediately watered it down to such an extent that it was effectively reduced to the direct election of a president and little else. Presidential powers were to be gradually reduced, the electoral system no longer included a two-round vote in the Electoral College and the post of premier reappeared surreptitiously within a semi-presidential shell. What emerged, then, was an unseemly mess. It is no wonder that this was immediately followed by the so-called professors' rebellion. The professors (among them Sartori, Pasquino, Augusto Barbera and Angelo Panebianco) signed an editorial of protest, demanding a new, coherent plan because the project by that stage had become as clear as mud.

Another example of Sartori's seminal influence at that time was the fact that first Massimo D'Alema and then Walter Veltroni, who were the leaders of the main left-wing party, the Democratic Party of the Left (PDS), asked him for a private meeting in order to benefit from his advice, establish rapport and ask for his support. It was the task of this writer, who in those years had responsibilities in the PDS, to prepare for Sartori's meetings with both leaders and to attend those meetings. During his encounter with D'Alema, Sartori put forth a proposal for a two-round electoral system limiting access to the second ballot to the leading four candidates in the Electoral College, but his proposal was not accepted.

Subsequently, while working on the D'Alema Bicameral Commission, this writer received from the then second in command at the PDS, Pietro Folena, the task of sounding out Sartori on whether or not he would be prepared to take on a formal role within the Commission (for example, by being appointed as a senator for life or by a special formal appointment based on nomination by the government). Sartori declined the offer, however, preferring to maintain his complete independence and freedom of conscience. It should be understood that had he accepted the offer, he would have received at the very least a nomination as a senator for life.

The centre-right also appealed to Sartori for assistance. In particular, Giuliano Urbani, one of his former students, a high-ranking parliamentarian, one of the founders of Forza Italia, a minister in the previous Berlusconi government and an influential member of the D'Alema Commission, repeatedly sought meetings and encounters with Sartori in order to obtain his assistance in smoothing things out within the Commission. On one occasion, in an attempt to overcome an impasse in the Commission's work, Urbani asked this writer to organise a trip by several Commission members to New York to meet with Sartori.

These events offer an idea of how important Sartori was in the first years of the transition from the First to the Second Republic. They testify to the expectations that the political establishment had for the celebrated scholar. This 'honeymoon' with the political leadership would only last until 1998. Up to that time or, more precisely, up until the failure of the D'Alema Bicameral Commission, the 'institutional reformers', who were mostly professors of political science and constitutionalists, had essentially marched in lockstep. A division then arose between those who supported a strong premiership (Barbera, Ceccanti, Fabbrini, Vassallo and Guzzetta) and those who opposed it (first Sartori, then Pasquino, Passigli, Bassanini, Cheli, Barile and Massari). For as long as they were united, the 'institutional reformers' had agreed upon a leading role for Sartori. However, the division among the reformers inevitably led to confrontations over various proposals. In addition, Sartori's hold over the centre-right completely vanished once the attempts at reform had failed. The Florentine scholar became an intransigent critic of Berlusconi's conflicts of interest, in a manner that only the old liberals such as Indro Montanelli and Federico Orlando could pull off. The long Berlusconi government of 2001–2006 governed under the newly approved electoral system, which was subsequently declared unconstitutional by the Italian Constitutional Court. The constitutional reforms were later rejected in a popular referendum. All of that served to dispel any possibility of reasonable institutional reform.

As a result, during what we might call the second phase of the Second Republic (since 1998), Sartori has assumed a position of continuous and indefatigable opposition to the status quo, providing critical, rigourous and biting opposition to various proposals and laws on institutional reform.

It should be mentioned that from the outset of the Second Republic, Sartori heavily criticised the main concepts, theories and institutions of the peculiar Italian 'majoritarian democracy', in particular the concepts of 'coalitional bipolarism' and the so-called mandate democracy. Whereas in the early years there had at least been some hope of enacting beneficial reforms, once this hope dwindled due to the ineptness of the political leadership, Sartori became the leading critic of the institutional, electoral and political structures of Italian democracy.

Let us take a look at Sartori's main criticisms by placing them into various thematic groups.

SARTORI'S CRITICISM OF THE INTERPRETATION OF MAJORITARIAN DEMOCRACY

For twenty years, an acute and incessant flow of criticism by Sartori, delivered with driving polemic force and vigour, addressed all of the main aspects of the new Italian democracy—from the introduction of the plurality system to the attempt to introduce a so-called strong premiership; from Berlusconi's role to his conflicts of interest; from the new personal parties to the more recent populist phenomenon of Beppe Grillo; from 'mistaken ideas on democracy' to a strenuous defence of the liberal features of democracy.

The overwhelming majority of the electorate rejected the proportional system in the 1993 referendum. Subsequently, a plurality system was adopted, which was labelled the *Mattarellum*[2] by Sartori. Finally, parliamentary elections were held (1994, 1996, 2001, 2006, 2008 and 2013) under the banner of bipolarism and alternation in government. Italy has witnessed a change from a proportional democracy to a majoritarian democracy.[3] The latter is understood not just as a democracy of alternating governments but as a distinct form of democracy that exhibits special characteristics. A peculiar vision of the culture of majoritarian democracy was firmly cast in ideological terms, which could not escape the harsh and continuous criticism of such an eminent scholar of democracy as Sartori.

Let us examine and briefly list the main characteristics of the majoritarian ideology:

- The proportional representation system is considered the source of all of the ills of the First Republic, from the absence of alternation to the overall degeneration of the political system;
- Whether the electoral system is first-past-the-post or proportional with a majority premium, it must guarantee bipolarism. This was done until 2001 by plurality vote and then through a majority bonus;
- In the new majoritarian democracy, it is the voters who directly choose the parliamentary majority, the government and the premier;
- Majoritarian democracy is, therefore, a 'mandate' or 'immediate' democracy (Duverger 1954), a democracy in which politicians derive their mandate to govern directly from the voters;
- Mandate democracy is incompatible with changes of the parliamentary majority, or so-called capsizing (*ribaltoni*);
- When a governing majority is interrupted, the country must vote again;
- The head of government cannot be changed because the voters have directly elected him or her. Berlusconi once said that whoever is directly elected by the voters is like 'someone anointed by the Lord' (La Stampa 2009);

- In the first-past-the-post system, 'winner takes all' and has the right to exercise power without compromises or mediation. This point has been particularly supported by Berlusconi and his group;
- Whoever is directly elected by the voters and thus receives a mandate to govern cannot be subjected to control by other powers, such as the judiciary system. Between the will of the voters and respect for the rule of law, it is the former that must prevail. This comes specifically from Berlusconi, who invokes this argument to evade judicial review of his actions;
- Conflicts of interest cannot be reviewed in mandate democracies because what counts the most is the will of the voters. This position, which naturally was fought for by Berlusconi, is to some extent shared or at least passively endured by the centre-left;
- Until 2008 political parties were considered an obstacle to the proper functioning of majoritarian democracy. Relations between politicians and the people should be direct and immediate, without intermediation by parties and the parliament. After 2008 Italy's two main leaders, Veltroni and Berlusconi, would concede that proper functioning of a first-past-the-post democracy requires majoritarian parties;
- After the window of opportunity for semi-presidentialism closed in 1998, the form of government most suitable for majoritarian democracy was considered to be the so-called strong premiership, characterised by direct election of the premier; the attribution of strong powers to him, including the power to dissolve the parliament and nominate/recall ministers, a strong majority bonus and prohibition of 'capsizing'; and no possibility to change the premier while the legislature is in session. If the premier must be sacked, the parliament must be dissolved, and new elections called;
- 'Majorititarian democracy' would no longer be a parliamentary democracy in the classic sense;
- The Westminster model and the example of other European majoritarian democracies confirms the 'presidentialist' trend, or rather the 'presidentialisation' of parliamentary systems, and confirms the interpretation of majoritarian democracy circulating in Italy.

It may seem like an exaggeration, but all of the points listed here have been made in the Italian debate on institutional reform and are supported across the political spectrum by the leaders of the main parties as well as a large group of constitutionalists, political scientists and news analysts.

Sartori has consistently railed against this ideology of full-blown majoritarian democracy in a manner that is consistent with his vision of democracy. Reading the titles of his writings on the subject is enough to understand the degree to which Sartori opposes the prevailing institutional theorising in Italy: 'Italy between Constitutional Errors and Blunders', 'The Fiasco of the Bicameral Commission', 'The Inability to Reform and Institutional Bastards', 'Towards an Unconstitutional Constitution?' (respectively, the appendices to the 1995, 1998, 2000a and 2004c editions of *Comparative Constitutional Engineering*), *Mala tempora* (Sartori 2004a) and *Mala costituzione e altri malanni* (Sartori 2006).[4] These titles give us a clear understanding of Sartori's intellectual position.

The fact is that Sartori's idea of democracy is the same as that advanced by the classic liberal-democratic thinkers over the past two centuries. His ideal democracy is certainly a representative one, as opposed to 'direct' democracy. It is a democracy that must protect its citizens from abuses of power by means of the distinct institutions and rules of liberal constitutionalism. Such a democracy should not subject itself to a sort of 'demo-power', which, in the absence of constitutional guarantees, can easily be transformed into a dictatorship of the majority. Or it can take on a form of populism known as 'direttismo', by which is meant a direct democracy void of all structures of intermediation, such as parties and parliaments. The power of the people in a democracy must be limited, never absolute, even when it is expressed by a majority of voters. The rights of minorities and individuals must be respected, no matter what the will of the majority is.

The 'liberal' component of 'liberal democracy' is both a condition *sine qua non* and also the element that defines democracy. The democratic component is a variable element, which may or may not exist. Liberal democracy is first and foremost 'demo-protection', the protection of the people from tyranny. Second, it is 'demo-power', the conferring upon the people of a part, even an increasing part, in the effective exercise of power. 'Demo-power is an added plus, which nonetheless cannot substitute for 'demo-protection', even if it presupposes that (Sartori 2008, 74–75).

It is *habeas corpus* democracy that interests Sartori the most. Deliberative democracy may lose strength as a consequence of a transformation of society and contemporary politics, but the protective democracy of individual rights must not falter. Likewise, it is the democracy of *Homo sapiens* that must be safeguarded and defended against attempts to empty it out from within through processes set in motion by the rise of *Homo videns*, as explained here:

> Anyway, 'the concern' . . . is this: that a *Homo videns* whose knowledge (actually mini-knowledge) does not go beyond what he sees on television, is not able to make a democracy work. Nowadays, democratic systems resist and, on paper, even spread, because in a secularised world that has rejected theocracy, an alternative principle of legitimacy does not exist. But with the exception of about a dozen countries (Italy excluded), democracies are emptied from within using a technique that I define as 'unconstitutional constitutionalism', because it is without adequate internal checks and balances. For this reason, I should add that I increasingly underline a distinction between democracy as 'demo-protection', in which the protection of the law exists, and democracy as

'demo-power', which is increasingly becoming *fictio iuris* and *fictio facti*. (Massari 2010, 319–20)

In conclusion, Sartori did not harbour any illusions about democracy, but he wholeheartedly agreed with the famous Churchill quotation that democracy is the worst political system, except for all the others. With respect to the various models of democracy (Sartori would prefer to talk of *types*), Sartori did not share Lijphart's 'anti-majoritarian obsession', nor did he concur in the exaltation of so-called consensual democracy or proportional democracy as superior forms. Even a majoritarian democracy is a fully consensual democracy. In fact, it probably has a greater need for consensus, given that under the 'rules of the game' it establishes that not everybody shares in power at the same time, although there is potential for alternation in who holds power. Therefore one should not speak of consensual democracy but more correctly of consociational democracy, which is the original, more correct term used by Lijphart (2001a).[5]

Sartori is not opposed to the concept of majoritarian democracy in theory. His criticism of Italianised majoritarian democracy does not result, therefore, from prejudice or bias. Majoritarian democracy is in his view fully representative parliamentary democracy. The usual consequences of majoritarian democracy—namely, alternation of power following electoral competition, the grant of immediate power to the party leader who obtains the majority of seats, the supremacy of the executive over the legislative branch—can certainly occur, but only when political conditions permit. It is uncanny that Satori, the greatest advocate for constitutional engineering and, more generally, for the practical application of political science, sees the limits to the applicability of majoritarian democracy. The Westminster model is precisely one example of this. Sartori is extremely clear-cut in affirming that this particularly British model—or rather prototype—of majoritarian democracy is not exportable or replicable by using the instruments of constitutional engineering:

> The problem is that the implantation of premiership systems largely defies constitutional engineering. (Sartori 1994, 136)

> ... So, the English premiership system can easily be destroyed while, on the other hand, it is not easy to obtain. Remember, on this score, that according to my laws on the effects of electoral systems . . . plurality elections cannot produce a two-party system unless the incoercible third-party electorates happen to be dispersed nation-wide at below-plurality levels—a hard condition for newcomers to meet. Therefore, any country that adopts a single-member district system with the argument that a premiership system of government would follow may be severely disappointed. (Sartori 1994, 104–5)

The Westminster model is based on a two-party system, which predates the adoption of plurality voting in single-member constituencies (Massari 1994b; Fisichella 2003). A two-party system cannot be created by simply adopting English first-past-the-post. This is precisely the enormous error that was made in Italy: the adoption of one-round plurality voting in 1994 occurred at the exact time that the party system was being destructed. In fact, without majoritarian parties, and with competition between two extremely broad and heterogeneous coalitions, the only possible result was an unseemly mess. Sartori is unflinching in his criticism of both *Mattarellum* and Italian-style bipolarism:

> With the Mattarellum party fragmentation has not been reduced (quite the opposite). . . . And the point is that the 1994 elections [but also those of 1996 and 2001] went exactly as should have been expected, or as foreseen by the 'laws' on the influence of electoral systems. . . . The 'law' says that single-member constituencies produce a two-party system at the national level if and only if those two parties are the only ones capable of winning in all circumstances. In Italy, this necessary condition isn't even remotely possible. . . . In fact, it is increasingly becoming even less possible because our majoritarian supporters also want to weaken the parties; and they don't understand that the weaker the parties are, the more impossible an English-style two-party system becomes. (Sartori 1995b, 222)

And yet there is more:

> None of our leading parties is capable of winning elections on its own in any electoral context. . . . [These parties] need allies. One percentage point makes the difference between winning and losing, what always happens is that almost all the small parties receive enough votes to make the difference between winning and losing a handful of seats . . . but when we move from a one-party majority to a multi-party majority—namely coalitions or cartels made up of several parties—the very notion of majority gets cloudy and, at the very least, is watered down. . . . But if the sum created is made up of heterogeneous and ideologically distant parties, then all we get is unwieldy stacks that do not form a majority . . . and these parties are fragmented at their core and at the mercy of small parties that are capable of paralysing the whole group. (Sartori 1995b, 223–24)

This is a realistic analysis and an irrefutable criticism of the extremely grave defects of the single-member, single-round system and the bipolar coalition that followed it. On the one hand, the *Mattarellum* was precisely the result of the blackmailing power of the small parties, which allowed them to 'negotiate for a share of the seats'. In effect, it increased the number of parties over those already in existence during the First Republic and thus managed to 'reproportionalise' what was supposed to be a majority system.[6]

On the other hand, it did indeed produce bipolar coalitions, but fragmented and heterogeneous ones.

In fact, all the electoral coalitions produced by the national elections in 1994, 1996 and 2001, each with a different composition, were either dissolved immediately after the elections or were succeeded by heterogeneous coalitions entirely typical of proportional democracies. In essence, Italian bipolarism is a totally artificial, forced and unnecessary construction, ours is a bipolarism that is rigid and restricted, for which each pole is a little fortress closed in upon itself (Sartori 2007).

Events have fully confirmed Sartori's condemnation. Yet it took over ten years for the main political forces to become convinced of the damage caused by the *Mattarellum*. The problem is that we've jumped from the frying pan into the fire. The new electoral law, which established a proportional system with thresholds for participation in parliament and a majority premium, was even worse than its predecessor.[7] All of its mechanisms and devices were worse than the ailments they were trying to cure: the majority premium at the national level for the House and the regional level for the Senate; restrictive thresholds for participation in Parliament that varied depending on whether or not the parties joined a coalition and that, in any case, conflicted with the majority premium; the identification of the leader of the coalition on the ballot; long, clogged candidate lists; etc. (Massari 2014c). It should also be noted that this law was designed in an attempt to safeguard a bipolarism that was in any event artificial, created as it was not by single-member constituencies but by a majority premium.

CONCLUSION

Giovanni Sartori was an uncompromising critic and polemicist of the Italian Second Republic for the over twenty years of its existence. He criticised the idea of majoritarian democracy, in practice and as imagined. What is more, Sartori criticised almost every electoral innovation and institution, from the attempt to surreptitiously introduce a strong premiership by means of identifying the candidate for premier on the ballot to the constitutional reform of 2005, which was later rejected in the 2006 referendum. He accompanied every step of the long Italian transition with critical commentary. Sartori directly and mercilessly criticised practically all of the political actors involved, from presidents of the Republic like Ciampi (see, for example, Sartori 2001) to the various prime ministers—Berlusconi *in primus*, but also Prodi and the various party leaders. One price he paid for all this was his occasional omission from the guest list for celebrations of the 2 June Republic Feast day at the Quirinale Presidential Palace, when Ciampi was president. (It should be noted, however, that Sartori was invited to breakfast by President Giorgi Napolitano in 2014 for his ninetieth birthday and was warmly received.)

It might be argued that Sartori's criticism, sometimes ironic, sometimes sarcastic and always biting, was the fruit of excessive polemical élan, in the vein of Curzio Malaparte's 'damned Tuscans'. That Florentine spirit is certainly the same one that has inspired various personalities from Machiavelli onward. Sartori had his own personal writing style, which was neither academic nor aseptic. His style was alive, vibrant, imaginative and given to posing paradoxes. Behind his journalism and even his pamphleteering stood logical reasoning that was rigourous and highly acute. The second life that Sartori lived—having transformed himself from a pure academic into a public personality—cannot be explained without reference to his prolific first one. Without the fifty years of indefatigable work that he dedicated to understanding democracy, its theoretical categories, its institutes and its assumptions, we would never have had the authoritative judgements he pronounced in his editorials. Behind each article lay myriad theories and empirical analyses and a huge amount of knowledge about comparative systems. A line of continuity runs between his scientific works on democracy and electoral and party systems and his critical writings on various issues in the Second Republic.

Another point needs to be emphasised: Sartori continually and strongly criticised his objects but did so almost always in isolation. In most cases, time and subsequent events have proved him right. This is what happened to his criticism of Israel's elected premiership, an innovation approved in 1992 that, although it was lauded by many Italian constitutionalists and political analysts, turned out to be a disaster and had to be annulled in 2001. The same was the case with the *Mattarellum*. In 1994 and 1995 Sartori was alone in his criticism, whereas most reformers offered it praise (to such an extent that they attributed its faults to the proportional threshold and not to the single-round system). It happened again with Sartori's criticism of Italian bipolarism. It took many years, but by 2008 many leaders and reformers had become convinced of the damage caused by enforced coalitional bipolarism. It happened with the *Porcellum* (the proportional system of representation with thresholds for participation and a majority premium). Bitterly criticised by Sartori from 2005, it was finally declared unconstitutional by the Constitutional Court in 2013. It happened with the constitutional reform approved by Berlusconi's centre-right majority, which consisted of a sort of strong premiership and a sort of federalism that was immediately labelled by Sartori as the 'unconstitutional constitution'. That reform was rejected in a popular referendum in 2006, for which Sartori was one of the leading promoters, together with a former president, Oscar Luigi Scalfaro, and the Astrid group, which included Franco Bassanini and Stefano Passigli. It happened with Sartori's unflinching condemnation of the Berlusconi phenomenon in its every aspect, from Berlusconi's conflicts of interest to his populism, from his continual attempts to create *ad personam* laws to his mode of government and his lifestyle, which Sartori went so far as to call a 'sultanate'. Most international public opinion came to the same conclusion as Sartori.

The list of these 'prophecies' could go on and on, prophecies that came true after a certain period of time. In this sense, Sartori was a remarkable forecaster of political reality. Many others, including worthy intellectuals, have simply been unable to predict the development of Italian politics accurately, even in the short run. Sartori's predictive ability with regard to the Second Republic disproves the old Hegelian axiom that all that is real is rational, and all that is rational is real. At the very least, that has not been the case in Italy during the Second Republic.

Giovanni Sartori was not only a great thinker and scholar but also a great fighter who never wavered in the defence of his ideas about democracy.

NOTES

1. This text is a modified version of my article, which appeared in *Contemporary Italian Politics* (Massari 2017).
2. Sartori was inspired by the name of the system's author, a Christian Democratic MP and the current Italian president, Sergio Mattarella. It was Sartori, in fact, who started to Latinise names in order to express irony and satire and to ridicule. This was the fate of the proportional electoral system, with its thresholds for participation in Parliament and a majority bonus that was approved by the centre-right majority in 2005. Sartori renamed it the *Porcellum* because the writer of the law, Roberto Calderoli, had himself termed it 'a dirty trick' (*una porcata*). Satori has coined a similarly colourful Latin name for every proposal on electoral reform, such as *Bastardellum*, *Manzellum*, *Proporzellum*, *Vassallum*, and finally *Italicum*, which is the latest proposal under discussion following an accord between Renzi and Berlusconi.
3. This is certainly what the promoters of electoral reform, the so-called institutional reformers, most of the political class and the public thought.
4. These last two volumes primarily contain his editorials in the *Corriere della Sera* over the course of 2004 through 2008.
5. For more on this topic, see chapter 7 of this book by Miroslav Novák.
6. It must be emphasised that Sartori was the very first person to direct this kind of criticism at the *Mattarellum*. Subsequently, the effective proportionality of the single-round single-member system would become widely accepted. There were still those who continued to attribute responsibility for the increase in the number of parties to the proportional aspects of the electoral system rather than to the single-round system and the blackmailing power the small parties enjoyed as a result of it.
7. The Calderoli law, called the *Porcellum* by Sartori, suffered from an original sin. It was designed and approved by the centre-right majority in 2005 at the end of the XIV legislature. The law had explicit aims and offered partisan advantages. The transition from a system based on single-member districts to a fully proportional one with participation thresholds, a majority bonus and closed party candidate lists was motivated by the fact that the centre-right coalition had always received (from 1994 to 2001) more votes in the proportional phase of the elections than in the majoritarian. Therefore both the single-member districts and the second-round ballot were eliminated.

Chapter Five

Giovanni Sartori and Party Theory

Klaus von Beyme

Giovanni Sartori had two main reasons for studying political parties. His interest in them derived from his interest in the wider context of how democracies function, especially in his native Italy. Sartori was also generally unsatisfied with the pioneering work of Maurice Duverger (1951) into political parties—he also often descended into polemics with Duverger—and with some of the then existing works on Italian party politics (see Pasquino 2009, 172; Sartori 1976, ix).

When it comes to party theory, Giovanni Sartori attained greatest influence with his *Parties and Party Systems: A Framework for Analysis* (Sartori 1976). In here, Sartori offered a wide-ranging theory of parties and party systems and, in particular, his very original and detailed typology of party systems. Obviously, Sartori was not only interested in party systems but in political parties as such. His work within party theory got, however, significantly interrupted by a petty crime. If we look at the original edition of *Parties and Party Systems*, we see that it was published as 'volume one'. 'Volume two' never followed. Why? What happened? Sartori did originally write two volumes of the book. In the first volume, published with Cambridge University Press and later reprinted by ECPR Press (Sartori 2005a), Sartori immersed himself into party systems and crafted the widely acclaimed typology mentioned earlier. It is here that Sartori also dwelled on how parties arise and how they are defined. Sartori decided to dedicate the second volume to classifications of parties and party functions and party organization. As he completed the draft of the 'volume two', it got stolen together with Sartori's car in the late 1970s, and he never found the energy to write it anew. While the story might at first appear banal, it had far-reaching consequences for his scholarship on (and our understanding of) political parties. Although Sartori supplemented some later editions of his book (mainly its Spanish translations), his take on the typology of parties, party organisation and functions never appeared in print in full.[1]

This chapter comes back to these 'stolen' issues from Sartori's pivotal work. Apart from taking us back to the specificities when it comes to research into political parties, this chapter offers an analysis of the development of political parties. The focus here is on their transformations in connection to various institutional matters, but even more so as a result of social, political and historical factors. Considerations of this 'sociological perspective', which are grounded in the wider theoretical context of scientific research into party politics, are therefore fleshed out with a number of examples from contemporary Europe, especially from Germany that I am most familiar with. While this chapter illustrates the influence of social and political factors on the development of parties, it also shows the extent to which Sartori's approach is still useful in the face of the ever-changing nature of politics and party politics.

RESEARCH ON PARTIES

Research on political parties has its specificities. First, parties are one of the few subjects which have been left almost exclusively to sociologists and political scientists for analysis. This resulted in a certain deficit in the existing studies on government and administration—a disadvantage that was overcome only when political science moved on from examining the institution of politics to scrutinising systemic outcomes in terms of policies. Even legal scholars interested in political parties—like Gerhard Leibholz, the influential German jurist—were only rarely interested in party theory (Leibholz 1958; 1965; Leibholz and Reif 1951).

Second, for a long time, research into parties had a poor reputation because it was not open to abstract theory. Classical works—from Ostrogorski (1903), through Michels (1911), to Duverger (1951)—were mostly typologies of political parties. Even comparative politics tended to classify political parties rather than to delve into quantitative research. Since the 1970s, behaviouralists and rational choice researchers corrected this drawback. The preferences of public servants from various parties were frequently studied not in a historical and empirical way but rather using models involving rational players and counter-players. Scholars who advocated this approach were more interested in predicting outcomes than in describing political reality. Theories of rational choice were fruitful, however, in examining the formation of coalitions and governments.

Third, in the 1960s and 1970s, parties were studied as part of interest groups and parliaments in order to suggest solutions to social and economic problems (Berger 1979, 30). This resulted in the fact that research into political parties became interesting to both the public and the media. Furthermore, in response to the student rebellion of the 1960s, the utility of parties became a topic of inquiry. Political parties were considered unavoidable, but they were not loved or trusted by large proportions of citizens they purported to serve (Mair 2008, 230). The importance of political parties combined with their rather low reputation made it possible for many political scientists to appear in interviews and as part of public roundtables. Sometimes this gave political scientists a bad name; political science seemed a form of journalism. Landslide victories by one party, for example, were frequently mistaken for a change in the party system itself. After a couple of years, the course of development normalised; *plus ça change—plus c'est la même chose.*[2]

Sartori was well aware of the problems connected with research into political parties and wanted to mitigate these issues. Here again, he expressed his conviction that political science should adopt a practical orientation. Sartori was skeptical about the quantitative and model-based analysis of parties and party systems, but he never slipped into simple 'reporting' in his texts, and this was a result of his terminological precision and his systematic view of party politics. Indeed, Sartori never succumbed to changing fashions when it comes to research. His 'qualitative' credo in research remained the same throughout his life:

> Words alone beat numbers alone. Words with numbers beat words alone. And numbers make sense or much greater sense within verbal theory. (Sartori 1976, 319)

What needs to be understood is that Sartori wanted to build a comprehensive theory of parties and party systems, which he described as a 'framework',[3] and for decades Sartori's typology of party systems—two-party systems, polarised pluralism and moderate pluralism—was a generally accepted 'framework'.

For Sartori, the most successful party system is based on a slight ideological distance between the major parties, an inclination to form coalitions between parties with different views and a predominantly centripetal competition among parties. An example of a country with a successful party system would be Switzerland, which never had polarised coalitions. Recently, however, ethnic parties and neopopulist groups have challenged the prevalence of centripetal competition (for example, Belgium, Great Britain, Spain and Italy). Some other recent movements overtook Sartori's assumptions: neofascist groups and communists are no longer as symmetrically positioned on the political spectrum as they were in Sartori's framework. Sartori's assumptions were sometimes guided by his distrust for the Italian Communist Party (PCI), although he recognised a trend in the PCI towards 'negative integration' into the party system of Italy. He also overlooked the fact that in Finland and

Iceland communists peacefully handed over power, proving that they had grown into integrated parties. On the whole, however, Sartori's classifications remained valid for several decades.

THEORY OF PARTY CHANGE

Sartori's work on parties contributed to a move from research based on a static view of parties to research into how parties change. Three stages in the development of political parties were discerned in the twentieth century: the era of ideological mass parties, the era of catch-all parties (*Volksparteien*) and the era of professionalised parties.[4] Elements of all three stages are found in most party theories, whether they rely on a model of integration or competition. The model of integration is oriented towards typologies. The competition paradigm—especially as it exists in the theory of elitist democracy in the school of Schumpeter (1942) and Downs (1957)—relies on models, offering a holistic approach to political systems.

Scholars who oriented their research on conflicts among parties (model of competition) considered their approach to be the only valid one for a long time. The transition from catch-all parties to parties of professional politicians took place after Sartori's time. Party financing gained importance, which it did not have when Sartori held sway over party theory. Party theory in the time of globalisation remarked upon a trend among citizens to individualisation that tended to make it more difficult for parties to influence individual voters by means of distinct ideology and party organisation. Identification with party, which was much emphasised by Sartori (1976, 328), is declining because of the deideologisation and individualisation of citizens. Therefore parties have invented counter-strategies. They are making their policies more flexible, commercialising party propaganda, professionalising their search for groups they can mobilise and turning to new media in order to contact possible supporters at home.

Media sometimes like to interpret a fluctuation of 5 percent in election results as a 'landslide change', and they frequently speak of a decline of parties and party disillusionment (*Parteiverdrossenheit*) among voters who have become tired of electoral campaigns. Political scientists, on the other hand, are rather astonished that party systems change slowly, over a long period of time. Fluctuations in support do occur, most frequently for the right or the left camp. That does not justify the 'nothing-new-under-the-sun approach' that sometimes appears in literature. Judgements about party change are frequently dependent on methodology. For instance, behaviouralists normally discover less dramatic change in their research. Sometimes they even do not agree with the widely accepted hypothesis of a 'decline of ideology' in party thinking, a decline that is particularly noticeable in the former communist countries of Eastern Europe.

Ideology today is less 'ideological' because it is concerned with certain policies and does not wage 'ideological crusades' any more. The ideologies and engagements of citizens concentrate on issues such as 'job creation' or 'environmental protection'. The only point of agreement between all the current schools of research into political parties is that membership in parties is declining (Schmitt and Holmberg 1995, 110). However, the same decline is visible among interest groups and churches.

We should also resist the temptation to construct a new universal party type, such as the 'cartel party' theorised by Katz and Mair (1995). The existence of this new type of party was soon challenged because of the static character attributed to it (Koole 1996, 520). Not all parties in a system belong to a 'cartel'. There is only a common interest in obtaining financial support from the state—about which there is hidden agreement among all parties, including ecology parties, right-wing populists and moderate communist groups.

SOCIOLOGY OF PARTIES AND PARTY ORGANISATION

Research of party politics is actually a competitive field. The main competition in party research takes place between enlightened institutionalists like Sartori and those who prefer a behaviouralist approach to the sociology of parties and party systems and—what is closely related to it—electoral systems.[5] Along with Sartori, Duverger, Lijphart, Rae and Rokkan were the premier researchers into party systems. Duverger (1951), Lijphart (1994) and Rae (1967) took the institution of electoral systems as a starting point and tried to explain its influence on party systems. Rokkan (1970), conversely, started from social cleavages and viewed electoral systems as a dependent variable. Sartori recognised the existence of electoral engineering in electoral systems as he evaluated the capacities of party organisations. He defended traditional institutionalist political science, referring to his personal experience with concrete historical and institutional facts—an approach dubbed by behaviouralists as 'impressionistic' (Sartori 1994, 36). He made fewer errors than those who attempted to analyse the same facts with mathematical precision. For Sartori, electoral systems are influenced by various factors, such as the system's social and regional structures, its degree of fragmentation, the extent of institutionalisation within it and the patterns of interaction among parties.

Intelligent voters, when taking for example Germany, anticipate the impact of their particular electoral system and vote in a strategic way. In systems that feature strong ideological conflicts, strategic and tactical voting behaviour is much rarer (Nohlen and Stöver 2010, 56).[6] Concentrating research on the limited calculations made by parties about the electorate's voting behaviour in the past few years has increasingly been challenged by the rise of unconventional forms of opposition from outside parliaments, through citizens' action groups and other public interest groups. This development may be dangerous for the following reasons.

First, certain militant groups can sometimes undermine decisions by a majority vote from the elections, which are essential to democracy. Second, individual groups that concentrate on achieving and maintaining a veto position and that have little interest in compromise can lay exclusive claim to representing the 'public welfare'. New movements calling themselves 'public interest groups' challenge equality of participation by citizens, one of the most important elements of modern democracy. Sometimes those groups continue to fight over an issue even when the parliament has already finally decided it—as in the case of the central rail station in Stuttgart.[7] Third, participation in unconventional, loose forms of organisation tends to be more selective than it is for conventional parties. Movements may try to advocate planning for groups that never before had participated in politics. Interests thus sometimes are no longer articulated within parties. Rather parties are considered the objects of influence seeking by new groups, smaller but better organised than the old parties.

Party change researchers that came after Sartori developed many hypotheses but obtained few results that have been proven true over time. Political parties have changed under the impact of new movements and are no longer catch-all, 'professionalized voter parties' (Beyme 2002). As I argue here, this is reflected in the following ways. First, social change has led to the individualisation of most citizens and to a certain degree has detached individuals from structural determinants in society. As a result, party membership is declining. Quantitative studies have shown, however, certain correlations between age, sex, educational level and occupation of actors in the public service and their inclination to engage in party activities (Biehl 2005, 220, 226).

Second, parties and interest groups are in a process of dealignment (as are, for example, the social democrats and the trade unions). In Germany the four old 'milieus' (Catholic, conservative-Protestant, Protestant-liberal and social democratic) are no longer decisive for the development of parties (Alemann 2000, 102). Especially in East Germany, the social milieus hardly exist as they do in the western part of the country.

Third, the change to a service-oriented society, especially a service-oriented society informed by mass media, has tranformed interparty competition. In former times, *Vorwärts*, the party newspaper of the Social Democratic Party of Germany (SPD), was essential reading for its members. In the new century, the newspaper has almost disappeared. The Catholic press also has little of the influence on the Christian Democrats that it had in former times. The income reporting of the two major parties in Germany shows that the Christian Democratic Union of Germany is increasingly dependent on grants from corporate donors. The SPD, on the other hand, has tried to compensate for its structural disadvantages by gaining influence over certain mass media outlets (Boll 2004, 24).

Fourth and finally, global trends such as extreme neoliberalism and a quasi-religious belief in the market (Leggewie 2013, 140) have radicalised voters who are abandoning the liberal centre and have enabled the rise of the right-wing populism that is challenging traditional party systems.

MUCH CHANGE, LITTLE DECLINE

The history of research into political parties is a history of past crisis scenarios. A quarter of a century after Sartori (1976) warned against polarised pluralism, nobody understood why. Perhaps this misunderstanding was due to the fact that Sartori was looking at developments between the two world wars and his classifications seemed sometimes outdated. Experience had showed that there has been much change but little decline in parties. Parties demonstrated that they were not completely helpless against negative tendencies, as has been shown also by recent analyses. Indeed, parties found organisational answers to preventing their decline. They made their policies more flexible, they commercialised their electoral campaigns and they increased their reliance on the media. The most successful parties agreed on the importance of concentrating their attention on voters, looking for realignment with interest groups, professionalising their leadership and allowing the 'etatisation' of party finance. Parties inside and outside parliaments changed their mutual relations in two ways. In the first place, parliamentary groups developed greater independence from their party leadership. Second, new media supported the transformation of visible parties into virtual ones.

During Sartori's time, scholars of parties examined the narrowing of ideological differences between families of parties. The social structures of voters and party members gained less attention, and the figures these researchers developed are hardly applicable today. 'Representation from above' (Esaiasson and Holmberg 1996) was strengthened in the era of professionalised voter parties. Voters did not require their elected deputies to represent their social class any more.

According to Olson (1965), parties do not follow the 'logic of collective action' as do interest groups. Barnes (1968, 121) was one of the last experts who tried to apply Olson's model of interest groups to party systems, albeit with limited success. Many organisational stimuli that motivate interest groups barely affect political parties, except perhaps for some of their leaders. Only party elites can advance their interests via party politics. Nevertheless, leadership positions within parties are becoming less attractive. Leading party functionaries are not well paid and mostly do not enjoy high prestige. Political amateurs at times compete with professional leaders. The size of the formal membership of parties does not play an important role in many countries. Especially in the United States, party identification is the functional equivalent of official membership.

While membership (and internal organisation of parties) may be one way to look at party change, the role of parties in the social environment offers yet another perspective. In pre-Sartori party theory, two approaches prevailed. The first took into account enduring loyalties among social groups. The other, using a social psychological approach, saw political parties as mere instruments for political socialisation, in competition with family traditions, peer groups, the media, schools, churches and other institutions. The first approach was relevant for long-term analysis; the second approach much better explained changes in the party scene over time, as new parties and new issues arose. Both approaches succumbed to the temptation of studying elections rather than parties as institutions per se. Lipset and Rokkan (1967) observed little fundamental change in parties between the 1920s and the 1960s. However, this 'nothing-new-under-the-sun approach' could no longer be supported. Denmark and the Netherlands soon provided a challenge to its validity. Notwithstanding, changes in political parties in Germany were explainable by 'borrowed votes' in some German Federal Laender in 2012. However, the *Mitteilungen des Instituts für Deutsches und Internationales Parteienrecht und Parteienforschung* published empirical evidence that suggested that this strategy did not work in the 2013 federal election, when the Free Democratic Party was voted out of the Bundestag (Hoffmann and Rosar 2013, 91). Only in the Netherlands did each new conflict create a new party. This caused much variation but hardly any change in the paradigm.

Postliberalism has led to a new form of social inequality. The counterreaction to that is the radicalisation of significant portions of the right wing of the Republican Party in the United States and of European right-wing populists (Leggewie 2013, 140). Threats from religious fundamentalism and terrorism are disturbing party systems to the extent that they no longer fit into Sartori's left-right framework. The new theoretical approach speaks of 'normal pathology' (Mudde 2010, 1179).

Cultural problems have often been more important than socioeconomic problems. At the same time, attitudes towards the welfare state have changed in populist movements, resulting in a form of 'welfare chauvinism' that seeks to reserve state subsidies for native populations. Welfare chauvinism argues that the welfare state no longer supports the 'common man' but rather bureaucrats and party elites. The French National Front (Front National) under Jean-Marie Le Pen, the Belgian Vlaams Blok and some Dutch groups have had some success with this idea in their countries. New orientations are also affecting the established parties. The demand side of the political process is a more popular topic in party research than the supply side. Attitudes have become more important than issues (Morlok and Poguntke 2012, 8). The traditional division of labour between parties and interest groups that prevailed through the twentieth century has been weakened.

Fortunately, new social movements that seek political autonomy instead of political representation have not yet been successful. Predictions that they would be have not come true. Earlier predictions of party theory that neocorporatism would lead to more functional representation—as once put forwards by Philippe Schmitter—were also less successful. Schmitter (2009) compared party researchers to a drunken sailor who looks for his lost key under a streetlight because the light is better, when he is well aware that he lost his key elsewhere along the road.

There is hardly any stable social milieu that offers new movements a lasting advantage over old parties in the current disintegrating social environment. No linear development of new theories has been successful. New issues are astonishingly quickly integrated into traditional party competition.

PARTIES IN POWER, COALITIONS AND POLICY OUTPUT

Alternation between internal change and external change was the predominant lens of inquiry in early party research. As change in party leadership does not necessarily lead to political innovation, alternation received less attention with time. Political events and pressure for adaptation should complete the scenario of innovation. The bottom-up principle holds that their social environment will change parties. The top-down principle, on the other hand, means that parties influence their societies. Parties in Parliament quite frequently indulge in 'representation from above' (Esaiasson and Holmberg 1996). Some parties want to maximize the number of offices they hold, while others try to influence the content of governmental policies. Changes in those targets of party policy were analysed in the rational choice debate (Strœm 1990). The logic of both of these approaches to coalition theory can be combined if we compare the offices normally occupied by party members. The literature on party change normally does not meet the scientific standards of the quantitative research applied to coalitions. Researchers came up with truisms, such as 'tactical adaptations are more frequent than revision of basic targets', because new programs are enormously costly to parties in terms of finances and time. Party members in democratic parties can have some impact on changes in their party's basic programs. Party leaders, however, normally make tactical adaptions, without consultation with the party base.

In postmodern times, according to Kay Lawson (1994), the search for power, even within parties, prevails over the power of belief. This dichotomy is probably too simple. Even political technocrats have to pretend they are promoting important policy goals. Only in Germany does Lawson's hypothesis seem to be true. Helmut Kohl and his faithful disciple Angela Merkel preferred a kind of 'democracy of coordination'. They waited until their party's factions, supported by the media, had ended their battles. They then reached a coordinated conclusion that they announced as their final decision. After 1998, Kohl's successor Gerhard Schröder, as an 'engineer of power', took a different tack and showed clear ideological leadership. This was only possible, however, when the two former factions of the SPD (Rudolf Scharping's and Oskar Lafontaine's) no longer enjoyed the support of party members, who were looking for a strong leader.

The conditions for gaining power in leading parties are difficult to generalise. Some scholars consider stable cabinets and the durability of leaders in office as the key variables (Fischer, Dowding and Dumont 2012, 514). Others consider the ability of parties to find a compromise important (Bellamy 2012, 480). Both sets of conditions are hard to apply in most European countries. The ideological factor was certainly weakened by an increasing 'migration of policy fashions', as happened in the sphere of environmentalism, peace policies and gender politics. Centralised parties were said to be less innovative than fragmented and decentralised ones. This was not always true, however. Willy Brandt was innovative because he had a centralised party behind him. A long period in opposition seems to increase a party's readiness for innovative policies (Bille 1997, 388). This was the case with the Labour Party under Tony Blair. The SPD's long period in opposition under Chancellor Kohl, however, did not create the same readiness for innovation. This can be explained by Germany's federal structure. Big parties are never completely doomed to the opposition because they may still govern important Länder such as North Rhine–Westphalia or Bavaria.

Innovation is sometimes carried out by strong parties, but they only rarely have decisive influence, as occurred when Charles de Gaulle created the Fifth Republic in France in 1958, and, in a less radical fashion, when the electoral law in New Zealand was changed in 1993. Some critics see a growing danger to democracy in the increasing power of party donors and in the support of parties by state budgets. Fortunately, all the predictions warning of 'authoritarian oligarchies' have not come true, with some exceptions, as in Hungary (Rathkolb 2011). The European Parliament elections in 2014 showed that increasing migration has strengthened radical right-wing populists not only in Switzerland (the Swiss People's Party) but also in France (the National Front, which finished first with 24.9 percent) and in Austria (Freedom Party of Austria, which pulled 19.7 percent of Austrians' votes). Other critics think that parties other than the new right-wing populists have less control over parliamentarians, activists, members and voters than they had in the early days.

Some critics even talk about 'ungovernability' because postmodern democracies have fewer stable majority governments. If we compare the period between the two world wars with the era after 1945, the latter period certainly saw more stable governments. Some countries like Denmark, Finland and Italy had experience with minority governments. However, this did not always lead to inefficient government in practice, as Denmark shows. Alternation has increased again recently. The problem is, however, that the margins between the left and right camps are normally so small that long-lasting, efficient policies are possible only in some European countries.

CONCLUSION

From a historical perspective, party research advanced a series of hypotheses that all proved wrong in the long run. Leftists who long issued polemics against 'catch-all parties without any political profile' have changed their minds after the failure of reideologization. Many former leftists ended up in 'professional framework parties' that had limited memberships and weak roots in new social movements, such as the Green and Environmental Parties. The decline of parties is a myth of party research. Few party systems ever broke down the way they did in Italy in 1994. Italy was a 'black Friday' event for many predictions because its system had theretofore been considered to be adaptive. Just as when communism broke down, all of a sudden everybody pretended to have known all along that it would happen.

The scholar who mentions many reasons has no decisive reason, Kant once said. To rephrase these words in the context of Sartori's work on parties, the search for an independent variable continues. Students of political parties who prefer quantitative approaches are devoted to this search, but they come to different conclusions in various countries and for different party families—and this includes groups that make up the parliamentary factions in the European Parliament. Popular literature does not, however, apply a high level of quantitative party research. It rather continues to offer a holistic approach. As already mentioned, Giovanni Sartori did not share the general appreciation of researchers for the rational choice debate. As he concludes in his seminal book,

> Models—as here understood—are supposed to predict trends, not single election. . . . [T]he best defense of the approach pursued here is in the point made by Downs himself (in spite of his deductive theorising), namely, that models should be tested primarily by the accuracy of their predictions rather than by the reality of their assumptions. (Sartori 1976, 351)

I could not agree more.

NOTES

1. Parts of it were later published in the form of a journal article (see Sartori 2005b).
2. 'The more it changes, the more it is the same thing'.
3. Whether he succeeded, especially given the theft of the 'second volume', remains a question.
4. Research on political parties entailed a wide discussion about the decline of political parties, evidenced by shrinking memberships, increasing volatility of vote totals and decreasing identification by citizens with parties. The 'étatisation' of parties was declared. On the other hand, the conception of professionalised 'cartel parties' (Katz and Mair 1995) was also criticised.
5. Empirically oriented researchers, who work with statistics, normally think that their approach is the only one that has developed party studies into a mature field of scientific inquiry (Shugart 2008, 25).
6. Because of his experience with such a system, Dieter Nohlen (2013), who is one of the most outstanding scholars on comparative elections, became an ardent follower of Sartori—without admitting it, however. Even more than Sartori, Nohlen, an exponent of the 'Heidelberg School', championed a historical-empirical approach to the study of party systems, without seeking quantitative correlations and clear causalities everywhere. Historical path analysis is increasingly popular in the comparative study of politics in Europe. Comparison shows very different historical developments between countries, leading to an open structure of competition in multiparty systems in the Netherlands and Denmark and more closed structures in Britain, New Zealand and Japan (until 1993), and in Switzerland and Ireland (until 1989) (Mair 1997).
7. This refers to the Stuttgart 21 project, which involved extensive reconstruction and modernisation of Stuttgart's main train station. The project represented a major intervention into the urban space of the town centre. Strong opposition to the project among the population escalated into massive demonstrations in August 2010. The controversy eventually led to the fall of the then existing coalition government of Baden-Württemberg and for the first time a Green Party took power in a German state. This forced partial changes in the plans, which were approved in a public referendum the following year, 2011.

Chapter Six

Sartori's Typology of Party Systems and Its Challenging Legacy

The Model of Polarised Pluralism and the 'Invisible' Politics

Maxmilián Strmiska

There is no need to stress here how much Sartori contributed to the formation of a general theory of political parties and party systems. The importance of Sartori's contribution has been recognised by a number of scholars (see, for example, Bardi and Mair 2008; Panebianco 2005; Pasquino 2005; Pappalardo 2005; and Klaus von Beyme's chapter in this volume could be added to the list). Equally appreciated has also been Sartori's typology of party systems, including its most interesting and original element: the model of polarised pluralism (Pasquino 2005; Sani 2005; Hanning 1984; Daalder 1983; Ventura 2016).

This chapter focuses on Sartori's theory regarding the interactions between 'visible' and 'invisible' politics in polarised party systems—a theory which has been largely ignored by scholars of politics. As I argue here, Sartori's approach to polarised pluralism retains its value even today. Sartori's thoughts on the systemic properties and mechanics of polarised pluralism present a challenging legacy that certainly deserves thorough and unbiased consideration by contemporary political scientists. Indeed, Sartori's approach here has far-reaching implications and serves as a point of departure that can be further elaborated in different directions by other scholars.

By pointing out the need to take into account cooperation and convergence among party elites as they pursue 'invisible' politics, Sartori challenged all existing typologies of party systems, including the one introduced by himself. My immediate goal is to show that this interaction is an essential component of his model, which explains the functioning and the durability of systems displaying polarised pluralism.[1] This component is also important because it helps to confirm the applicability of his model to the Italy of the period from the mid-1960s to the early 1990s. It assumed new importance in 1992 when the Italian party system collapsed in the wake of revelations about the impact of 'invisible' politics. It provided a weapon for Sartori to wield in his defence of the analytical and predictive ability of his model of polarised pluralism. Any assessment of the role of 'invisible' politics and the interplay between 'visible' and 'invisible' politics is controversial, both analytically and normatively. It goes far beyond an 'esoteric', purely academic discussion of Sartori's model of polarised pluralism.

THE MODEL OF POLARISED PLURALISM AND ITS LEGACY

Sartori developed his model of polarised pluralism in several phases over time. Its precise temporal history is somewhat complicated because it was elaborated at different points in time, in Sartori's first and last writings on the topic, which were published in Italian (1963–1984) and in English (beginning in 1966 and culminating in 1976). Sartori's 'mature' conception of polarised pluralism is expressed in his 1976 book *Parties and Party Systems* (Sartori 1976; cf. 1966a; 1982; 1984; 2005a) and had the most impact in the wider international context.

Sartori's early conception identified three basic characteristics of polarised (or 'multipolar extreme') pluralism: multipolarity (or more precisely tripolarity, including the centre) of the party system, centrifugal party competition and an overall 'nonmoderate' or extremist nature (Sartori 1966a; 1982, 61–62, 89). In his extended version of the model, produced in the 1970s, Sartori set forth no less than eight principal properties of polarised pluralism. These include (1) the presence of anti-system parties, (2) the existence of 'bilateral' opposition parties, (3) the centre positioning of one party or group of parties, (4) a high degree of polarisation, or major ideological distance, between parties, (5) the predominance of centrifugal trends over centripetal trends in party competition, (6) ideological differences between parties and society, (7) the presence of irresponsible opposition forces and (8) the existence of a politics of triumph. In what follows I will briefly elaborate on each of these principal properties.

First, Sartori distinguished between a broad and a strict definition of an 'anti-system' party. The intensity of a party's 'anti-attitude' can vary. His broad definition included all political parties with a common denominator—their delegitimising impact on the system. A party can be considered anti-system if it undermines the legitimacy of the regime it opposes (all protest parties could be included here). On the other hand, Sartori limited his strict definition to anti-system parties that seek to change not only the government in office but the very system of government itself because they do not share the belief system and the values of the existing political order. An anti-system party in the strict sense upholds an extraneous ideology and confronts the prevailing polity from the maximum of ideological distance (Sartori 2005a, 117–18).

When it comes to the existence of 'bilateral' opposition parties, second, Sartori identified two poles of opposition in polarised pluralism that are mutually exclusive and that are each closer to the governing parties than they are to each other. They are thus 'counter-oppositions' that are mutually incompatible.

With regard to the centre positioning of one party or group of parties, third, Sartori noted that in polarised pluralism the party system has a triangular formation (instead of the classic bipolar left-to-right spectrum) with multipolar competition hinging on a centre that must contend with both a left and a right wing. The Christian Democracy Party in Italy was an illustrative example. It occupied the political centre and rendered the whole party system of the 'first' Italian Republic 'immobile'.

Fourth, in polarised pluralism, according to Sartori, there are very deep ideological cleavages between parties, a low degree of consensus and widely held doubts about the legitimacy of the political system. This results from the occupation of the political centre by a party or parties and immobility of the system. Ideologically diverse parties are discouraged from pursuing centripetal convergence (Sartori 2005a, 120).

Fifth, Sartori predicted that centrist parties would lose votes to one or both extremes in a system of polarised pluralism. According to him, the classic example of a centrifugal trend was the 'first' Italian Republic, with its eroding majority coalition of centrist parties and steady growth of the extremes in the 1970s.[2] As mentioned, Sartori's most famous book, *Parties and Party Systems*, was published in 1976. His analysis of the Italian party system did not anticipate the demise of communism and the transformation of neofascists into a standard conservative party, which emptied both extremes of the Italian party system in the 1990s. Of course, the centrist hegemon at the time, Christian Democracy, did not survive the fall of the 'first' Italian Republic either.

Sixth, Sartori understood ideology as a particular mentality—a distinctly doctrinaire, principled and high-flown way of focusing on political issues. He believed that the common characteristic of political parties is that all of them fight each other with ideology regardless of their 'ideological temperature'. Sartori asserted that the more pluralism is polarised, the more smaller parties fight for their survival by indoctrinating their followers as 'true believers'. In the case of Christian Democracy, he showed how that could even apply to the largest party in the system (Sartori 2005a, 121–22).

In polarised pluralism, seventh, there are no alternative coalitions but the presence of irresponsible opposition forces. The centrist party is necessarily destined to be part of any possible governmental majority. On the other hand, the extreme anti-system parties are by definition excluded from alternation in office, which leads them into irresponsibility as an opposition. According to Sartori, the less a political party expects to be part of government, the less responsibly it behaves.

The existence of a politics of triumph forms the eighth and last principal property of polarised pluralism for Sartori. In polarised pluralism, parties tend to overpromise and to dramatise the political struggle, reinforcing a trend from 'responsible' competitive politics to unfair competition (Sartori 2005a, 123–24).

Sartori clearly viewed polarised pluralism as the worst possible variant of competitive party arrangements. He considered it a 'hardly viable' system that favours extremist politics. He believed that it pushes the dominant party's elites towards semiresponsibility in power and the anti-establishment party elites towards complete irresponsibility. Such a system is unable to cope with explosive or exogenous crises. According to Sartori, the Italian system was not totally impotent, yet it had no positive aspects. It could not be reformed (and in fact, the reforms that were implemented were wrongly conceived and on the whole unsuccessful). Soon or later, such a system must end up in sheer paralysis or 'deflagration' (Sartori 2005a, 130–32).

It should be stressed that Sartori was very consistent in developing his model of polarised pluralism. He drew upon a series of assumptions that he never abandoned. Neither did he stray from the basic direction and manner of his argument. However, Sartori's consistency was not an asset in all respects. Sartori's position—at least from 1976—can be perceived as an obstinate refusal to change anything in his basic conception of the politics of polarised pluralism. In spite of growing criticism with regard to the applicability of his model to the Italian context, Sartori believed that it was valid as it was. His arguments were tainted with a markedly defensive and apologetic tone.

The consistency of Sartori's conception of polarised pluralism and the tenacity and dynamism of his defence of his model cannot be fully understood without reflecting on the debate that it provoked in Italy and its close relationship to the Italian political context. Is there any added value in examining that context from an analytical point of view? Well, it depends. The extent to which the arguments used in the previously mentioned debates really addressed the principal points of Sartori's model of polarised pluralism and his typology of party systems as a whole is worth considering. The point is that those discussions were mostly dominated by arguments about what was 'politically relevant' or directly applicable to the anti-system nature of the communist opposition. Less attention was paid to such issues as centrifugal trends in party competition or the concept of the 'centre' and its role in the party system.

Sartori's model of polarised pluralism was subjected not only to criticism but also exposed to direct competition by other theories of the nature of the Italian party system and the direction in which it was evolving. The first and longest-lasting competitor to Sartori's model was Giorgio Galli's conception of the Italian party system as 'imperfect bipartism' (Galli 1966; cf. 1972; 1975; 1983; 1991). Galli concentrated on the position and role of the two major Italian parties, Christian Democracy (DC) and the Italian Communist Party (PCI) in a context in which the DC never alternated in power with another party and the whole political system was rendered immobile. Unlike Sartori, Galli allowed more space in his conception for the role and position of the PCI. In his view, the relationship between the DC and the PCI was stable and basically under control, not one that would lead to inevitable and ever-growing conflict. As a result, in the eyes of both experts and the general public in Italy, Galli's reassuring but 'very simple theory of imperfect bipartism' (Sartori 1982, 193) could easily compete for influence with the much more elaborate Sartorian model of polarised pluralism.

A remarkable and constructive contribution to the discourse on the nature of the Italian party system was that of Paolo Farneti, the author of the model of 'centripetal pluralism'. Farneti proposed his model as complementary to Sartori's conception. According to him, Sartori's polarised pluralism could effectively be used to interpret the evolution of the Italian party system until the mid-1960s. The period that followed (until 1979) required a different model, that of centripetal pluralism (Farneti 1993, 217). Farneti believed that centripetal pluralism had a number of features in common with polarised pluralism, such as the presence of relevant anti-system parties, the absence of full alternation of parties in government and the nonhomogeneity of the 'centre'. The principal difference between Farneti's theory and that of Sartori was the absence of any endemic trend towards a destabilising radicalisation and politicisation of the electorate. Farneti believed centripetal pluralism is normal where a centrist, moderate electorate is relatively stable, allowing for long-term sustainability of the balance of power (and of electability) between pro-regime governmental parties and more or less antiregime opposition formations. In Farneti's model as applied, the main Sartorian anti-system actor, the Italian Communist Party, is a 'pro-system' extreme party and the Italian Social Movement (MSI) is an 'irrelevant' party, applying Sartori's definition of relevancy. The whole system thus avoids extreme polarisation and becomes centripetal, not centrifugal (Farneti 1993; Mastropaolo 1993).

The most innovative element in Farneti's approach (which he developed from the early 1970s; see Mastropaolo 1993) was the stress he placed on a prevailingly centripetal orientation of the Italian party elites, which sought to compensate for polarisation at the 'mass level' (or rather, for the consequences of the previous polarisation of the masses). In short, Paolo Farneti was aware that a party system cannot remain polarised ad infinitum and that radicalisation cannot be an endless source of political power. There was a need to explain how the Italian party and political system could 'survive' its long-term polarisation and why it had not collapsed long before. Even though he was not explicit, he challenged Sartori's model of polarised pluralism as a whole by pointing out that it did not completely explain the Italian reality.

POLARISED PLURALISM AND 'INVISIBLE' POLITICS

Sartori was well aware that Farneti's conclusions touched upon a delicate point in his conception of polarised pluralism (Sartori 1982, 320–22). It was critically important to explain how a system of polarised pluralism could survive in spite of the clearly self-destructive 'evolution logic' intrinsic to Sartori's model. Sartori's effort to elaborate upon and beef up his theory of the delegitimisation and relegitimisation of parties operating in a polarised party system should be appreciated in this context. He had to explain the relationship between delegitimisation and relegitimisation. He also had to solve a specific puzzle: how to defend his belief that the principal features and basic qualities of the Italian party system, which he considered to be the very embodiment of polarised pluralism, still validated his model even in the absence of constantly escalating extremist politics. Precisely in order to solve that puzzle, Sartori began to focus on 'visible' and 'invisible' politics and their interplay.

According to Sartori, 'visible' politics involves open, public political action, especially representations and promises made by politicians for the mass media, while invisible politics consists of back-room deals and mouth-to-ear communications. He directly associated 'invisible' politics with money, spoils, clienteles and dirty deals. However, his conception of 'invisible' politics is broader than that (Sartori 2005a, 143–45). His argumentation was somewhat ambivalent, however, and leaves space for diverse analytical and normative implications. We should therefore use a fair bit of caution in drawing conclusions. It is quite clear that Sartori did not want to take a normative approach to the difference between visible and invisible politics.[3] He was mainly concerned with visible politics and its relationship to the electorate and with invisible politics pursued by party representatives at the parliamentary and leadership levels. In his view, the latter form of politics involves acts of pragmatic bargaining that are feasible only under cover of invisibility. Sartori underlined these different forms as a starting point for defining a subsidiary feature typical of polarised pluralism, the 'inconvertibility' of 'visible' and 'invisible' politics.

In Sartori's view, the gulf between 'visible' and 'invisible' politics and their inconvertibility are a product of the excessive ideologisation of polarised polities. Ideological goal setting creates a vicious circle in which party leaders become 'prisoners of their own image-selling' in the long run (Sartori 2005a, 133, 137–44). This failing limits certain things Sartori considers important: pragmatic cooperation and mutual relegitimisation of party elites at a less visible level. According to him, cooperation and relegitimisation is the solution to the puzzling lack of extremism in Italian politics. He believed that if the polity under scrutiny is centrifugal at all levels (electoral, parliamentary and party leadership), then it is doomed and inevitably must end up in 'deflagration'. On the other hand, he also believed that a system of polarised pluralism can endure if the centrifugal tendencies of electoral competition in polarised pluralism are diminished and moderated by centripetal convergence among party elites practicing 'invisible' politics. That is to say, the system's survival depends on what is happening at its different levels. The covert cooperation and hidden pragmatism of elites is enough to prevent the collapse of the system—but nothing more than that. They are too little to allow for its transformation. The elites in power dare not exceed a certain limit as they implement a *conventio ad excludendum* against the elites of antiregime parties. Although antiregime elites are often far from being as antiregime as they seem, they cannot admit that in public and they act accordingly. Sartori's fragile and—in view of his original assumptions—somewhat meandering argument was his way of defending his model of polarised pluralism. It was his attempt to fit the reality of Italian politics into his model's characteristics 'as they have been described' (Sartori 2005a, 145; cf. Sartori 1982, 223, 323).

Nevertheless, despite Sartori's best efforts, he could not effectively defend his model of polarised pluralism in its entirety, including its claimed predictive ability. The question arises: To what extent did Sartori's defence of his model contribute to the development of a conception of polarised party systems with broader implications for his typology of party systems as a whole? It probably could have, but Sartori did not take that direction. Nothing indicates he ever had such intent. In evaluating the interplay of 'visible' and 'invisible' politics, he did not discuss the threat of an explosive endogenous crisis if 'making of the invisible visible' revealed that the true behaviour of party officials at different levels differed from their rhetoric to such an extent that the mass of the electorate would refuse to tolerate it. Sartori thus failed to use the controversy over his model to sharpen its analytical and predictive capacity, which would have been extremely important and useful in the 1990s. All of this allows a better understanding of why Sartori's conception of polarised pluralism came under severe criticism after the collapse of the Italian party system in 1992–1993.

The noted Italian sociologist Alessandro Pizzorno explicitly rejected both Sartori's model of polarised pluralism and his entire approach to the study of the role of parties and party arrangements. He believed that Sartori made a basic mistake by taking everything party actors said about themselves for granted, judging them by their words and not by their actions (Pizzorno 1994, 285). That was, Pizzorno wrote, the biggest illusion of the party politics of the 'first' Italian Republic. Many scholars, Sartori included, did not notice the 'strange' but close relationships between all political actors that contradicted their purported ideological distance. In other words, in Pizzorno's opinion Sartori mistakenly emphasised 'visible' politics at the expense of 'invisible' politics. The latter was of critical importance for understanding the nature and functioning of the whole political polity. While Sartori's polarised pluralism was predictive at the level of 'visible' politics, Pizzorno contended that 'invisible' politics was dominated by 'hidden consociationalism' (*consociativismo coperto*). Consociationalism could only work covertly, with a good cover story—illusory ideological disagreement.

Pizzorno considered this 'hidden consociationalism' to prevail in most Western democracies, where 'no irreducible political identity is at stake and political demands all become negotiable. Interest groups asking for specific policies are the main actors on the political scene whereas the political parties tend to lose their programmatic and organisational identity' (Pizzorno 1981, 272). Pizzorno also believed strong, ideologically competing parties were a temporary phenomenon:

> Stable electoral cleavages, and clear alternatives in party programme are more likely to be found in periods of intense social (mainly occupational and geographic) change and of consequent strong pressures by new categories of interests to enter into the political system. If this hypothesis is true, strong parties, with clearly delineated programs and integrated membership, are a temporary phenomenon. They emerge both to strengthen and to control the access of the new masses into the political system and become redundant once both entry and control are achieved. If they are typical of pluralism, then, they are typical only of its first phase, when big collective actors are admitted sharing power into a system of representation. (Pizzorno 1981, 272)

Following up on this premise, Pizzorno analysed the party system of the 'first' Italian Republic, which he saw was dominated by a few political parties that managed to agree among themselves without too many qualms. Unlike Sartori, he did not consider the Italian Communist Party an anti-system political party. Sustained periods in office by PCI members at the regional level during the period of the *compromesso storico* in the 1970s had tempered the PCI's exclusion from Italian national governments (Mair 1997, 41).[4]

Pizzorno believed that Italian intellectuals—including Sartori—perfectly satisfied their need for a pretext with the previously mentioned illusory ideological disagreement. They were providing the political discourse with precisely the definitions and models they needed. They regarded political actors as highly as they regarded themselves and helped them to retain their public prestige (Pizzorno 1994, 288, 291–92, 294). Pizzorno's sharp criticism of Sartori's conception of polarised pluralism was a remarkable highlight of the Italian debate of the time about that model, but it failed to put an end to discussion of the subject (cf. Lanzalaco 2012; Ventura 2016; Ignazi 2017).

It should be noted that the interplay of 'visible' and 'invisible' politics continues to be part of academic debate, but that debate no longer concerns itself with explaining the survival of polarised party systems or with the interactions of party elites on the invisible (private) level. A telling recent example of the current debate is provided by Piero Ignazi. Ignazi conceives of 'invisible' politics primarily as intraparty or 'esoteric' politics. To him it is a fundamental reason for the rise of anti-system parties (Ignazi 2017, 270).

CONCLUSION

I hope these lines have shown that Sartori's theories of the behaviour of party elites on the level of 'invisible' politics and—broadly speaking—of the relationship between 'visible' and 'invisible' politics were minor, subsidiary elements of Sartori's model of polarised pluralism, yet they were important ones. In dealing with the subject, Sartori made a series of assumptions (including the idea that 'less ideological' necessarily means 'less irresponsible'). He pursued the objective of maximally defending the prestige of his model of polarised pluralism. From today's point of view, however, the mere fact that he discussed the subject is more important than how he did it or the context in which he did it. Polarised pluralism is a theory with far-reaching implications, which can be elaborated upon in different directions, even though that does not seem to have been Sartori's primary intention. By pointing out the need to take into account cooperation and convergence among party elites practicing 'invisible' politics, Sartori challenged all typologies of party arrangements including his own. That in itself is a good reason to read (and reread) Sartori's works.

NOTES

1. This component of Sartori's theory can be viewed as a 'protective shield' for the core assumptions of his model of polarised pluralism (cf. Lakatos 1989). It is, of course, not the only possible view.

2. The Italian Communist Party peaked at 35.3 percent of the vote and the Italian Social Movement at 9 percent.

3. However, it should be remarked here that some of Sartori's statements and definitions can be understood as an opening to politically salient and distinctively normative interpretations of the difference between 'visible' and 'invisible' politics. This seems to be the case, for example, with Sartori's description of 'visible' politics as the 'democratic level' of politics (Sartori 1974, 682; cf. Sartori 1982).

4. The 'historic compromise' was proposed in 1973 by Enrico Berlinguer, General Secretary of the PCI, as a 'democratic alliance' with Christian Democracy. The peak of cooperation happened in the second half of the 1970s, when the PCI provided external support to a one-party Christian Democracy government led by Giulio Andreotti. After the kidnapping of Aldo Moro and a subsequent increase in anticommunist sentiment, the compromise was discontinued in 1980.

Chapter Seven

Is the Consensus Model of Democracy Better for All Countries?

On Sartori's Critique of Lijphart

Miroslav Novák

Giovanni Sartori long stressed the danger of terminological camouflage and conceptual stretching in comparative politics (Sartori 1991a). In his critical analyses, Sartori also examined certain concepts that Arend Lijphart used in formulating his dichotomous typology of democracies (majoritarian and consensual). In this chapter, I will show how Sartori developed his critique of the concepts employed by Lijphart. I will then compare Sartori's critique with my own and fit both of our critiques into the usual framework for discussion of the consensus model of democracy.[1] I must warn that both Sartori's critique and my own relate primarily to Lijphart's later conception of two models of democracy (consensus and majoritarian) and only secondarily to his idea of consociational democracy, which is one element of Lijphart's earlier theory of four types of democracy.[2] Like Sartori, I believe that elaborating consociational democracy as a type was a useful contribution to empirical research into democracy. However, Lijphart's normative dichotomy between two models of democracy is more problematic. One of them (consensual democracy) Lijphart approves of and urges upon all democratic countries, while the other (majoritarian democracy) Lijphart criticises and discourages all democratic countries from applying it.

SARTORI AND LIJPHART'S MODEL OF DEMOCRACY

In his 1987 work *The Theory of Democracy Revisited*, Sartori regarded the dichotomy between Lijphart's two models of democracy as overstated:

> A first observation is that I would stress the ideal-type, indeed the polar-type, nature of the distinction between majoritarian and consociational democracy. Lijphart stresses, instead, the empirical and empirically extracted nature of his types and, by so doing, is in danger of overstating his case. The contrast is empirically overdrawn, to begin with, in that no real-world democracy abides by absolute majority rule. (Sartori 1987, 239)

From there it is only a small step to rejecting the term 'consensus model' of democracy altogether:

> In his most recent volume, *Democracies* . . . , Lijphart changes 'consociational democracy' into 'consensus democracy'. I shall not follow this renaming since it may convey, if unwittingly, the idea that the Westminster, majoritarian model is not consensus-based. (Sartori 1987, 251)

The German political scientist André Kaiser (1997, 433) similarly states: 'Lijphart underestimates the fact that a minimum of consensus is vital for both types of democratic systems'. Maurice Duverger (1988, 42–43) went even further: 'Consensus turns its back on centrism because it [consensus] is a necessary condition for alternation'.[3] Sartori himself extended his views in his 1994 work *Comparative Constitutional Engineering*:

> The contrast [between the majoritarian and consensus models] is biased because its wording conveys, rightly or not, that majoritarianism maximizes conflict or, at any rate, handles conflict poorly. I would say, instead, that consensus management is the very essence of all democratic governance, and that there is no a priori reason for holding that the Westminster method cannot handle the consensus-conflict maze as well as, or even better than, the consensus-consociational method. Indeed, Lijphart's argument can be turned around all the way. By facilitating something you make it happen. The more you give in, the more you are asked to give. And what is not discouraged becomes in fact encouraged. If you reward division and divisiveness (and this is precisely what *proporz* and veto power do), you increase and eventually heighten divisions and divisiveness. In the end, then, Lijphart's machinery may well engender more consensus-breaking than consensus-making. For peace at all costs is the worst possible way of averting wars. (Sartori 1994, 72)

I would like to emphasise one point in Sartori's analysis that seems especially important to me: the minority veto. 'Finally, to admit the minority veto as a major and normal means of limiting power is to admit a shuddering principle' (Sartori 1994, 71–72). Lijphart (1992, 216–17, 220) contended in one of his essays from 1992 that the Czechoslovak federation after 1989 was an example of a consociational democracy. At the same time, the veto power wielded de facto by the Slovak minority was available thanks to symmetrical bicameralism (Lijphart 1992, 217). But precisely this minority veto is considered by some specialists as one of the factors that contributed to the breakup of federal Czechoslovakia.[4]

Sartori further describes serious problems arising from the combination of a parliamentary system with symmetrical (or strong) bicameralism (a two-chamber parliament, in which both chambers possess equal power). Yet it is just this combination of parliamentarism and symmetrical bicameralism that Lijphart recommends.

Lijphart argues that

> parliamentarism and strong bicameralism are incompatible only if cabinets tend to be formed based on narrow majorities in the first chamber. If cabinets are grand coalitions, they will have no problem. In fact, the obvious solution to the problem of 'two mutually hostile majorities' in a strong bicameral legislature is to form an oversized coalition cabinet. (Lijphart 1984, 104)

Sartori rightly rejects Lijphart's 'solution':

> But here Lijphart belittles the problem and—I am afraid—ultimately misses its intractability. Sure, a grand coalition may be a way out—but almost always a poor one. For minimum-sized coalitions generally are more homogeneous than oversized ones; and this implies that in order to avoid a government-parliament deadlock we may create an intra-governmental deadlock (among mutually dissonant and litigious partners) that is just as unworkable. (Sartori 1994, 186)

According to Sartori, Lijphart's passage from his specific theory of four types of democracy (to repeat: centripetal, centrifugal, consociational and depoliticised) to his grand general theory of two models of democracy (consensus and majoritarian) is mostly terminological:

> Consociational democracy is rebaptised 'consensus democracy' and while the consociational construct presupposed a segmented social structure, the new name for this hinterland is 'plural societies'. Futhermore, the initial construction was typological: consociational democracy was a 'type'. Consensus democracy is displayed, instead, as a 'model'. Types we know how to handle (logically and methodologically). Models we do not even know what they are, but they are assumed to be entities of a much more majestic status.
>
> Now, to change a word is not simply to change a word: it changes a meaning. Words have semantic projection, they convey interpretations. Thus, if we say 'consensus democracy' we already have in our hand of cards the winning trump. Can anybody ever hold that a non-consented democracy is as good as a consented one? Likewise, if we say 'plural societies'—indeed a very

bland and diluted labelling—the suggestion that inevitably creeps into our minds is that since all societies are, in some manner and to some extent, plural, then Lijphart's recipe is indeed good for all societies. (Sartori 1994, 70)[5]

Thus, we arrive at the key point, which Sartori formulated this way:

> In winding up, Lijphart smoothly and almost imperceptibly leads us from the thesis that consociational democracy is best for segmented, heterogeneous and/or polarized societies, to the utterly different thesis that it is a superior 'consensus model' for virtually all societies. But no. . . . Thus, I subscribe to the first formula, but cannot subscribe to the second one. (Sartori 1994, 72)

POLARISATION, SEGMENTATION AND HETEROGENEITY

Here it is necessary to distinguish between two things: segmentation (or put more simply but less precisely, heterogeneity) and polarisation. Is consociational democracy capable of resolving only the problems of heterogeneous and/or segmented societies or can it also solve the problems of a polarised society? According to Sartori, it can in fact solve the problems of heterogeneous and segmented societies, but not (and here he differs significantly from Lijphart) the problems of a polarised society. Sartori developed this thesis in the framework of his typology of party systems, particularly in his famous essay 'Polarization, Fragmentation and Competition in Western Democracies', whose co-author was Giacomo Sani.

For Sartori, this question is entirely fundamental because his key distinction between the two main types of multipartism (moderate pluralism and polarised pluralism) depends on how it is answered. It could be that the fragmentation of party systems can stem either from segmentation (simply put, from the heterogeneity of a society) or from polarisation. Each alternative, however, leads to a completely different result: in the first instance to 'moderate pluralism' and in the second to 'polarised pluralism'. Whereas the first of these is functional, solid and stable, the second is dysfunctional, vulnerable and unstable. Sani and Sartori said: 'It is doubtful that the "consociational democracy" experiment can be successful in systems that have high polarization' (Sani and Sartori 1983, 308). Together with Sani, Sartori developed his argument a bit further:

> The argument has been made that not only fragmentation but also polarization can be managed 'consociationally'. It is not clear whether the proponents of this view distinguish between fragmentation and polarization. But if the distinction is drawn, and if it is understood that the key variable is polarization, then we have no convincing evidence that consociational elites may overcome a state of extreme polarization. To be sure, what has not happened in the past may still happen in the future. Yet the hypothesis that polarization can be

cured by consociational practices is somewhat self-contradictory, for the counter-argument might well be that a state of polarization points to, and results from, conflict-seeking and intrinsically hostile elite orientation. (Sani and Sartori 1983, 336)

In short, the 'consociational democracy', which key element is the proportional representation, is not capable of resolving the problems of a polarised society, but on the other hand 'some form or other of the double ballot can be smoothly applied even to highly polarized settings' (Sartori 1994, 69).

Sartori (1994), in *Comparative Constitutional Engineering*, further demonstrates that Lijphart in his newer conception of two models of democracy—as opposed to his older theory of four types of democracy—is using diluted concepts. Sartori's observation is undoubtedly correct, but I believe that Lijphart has also some good reasons. 'Consociational democracy', which is the best-known type from Lijphart's old empirical typology of democracy, is itself a construct dating from the second half of the 1960s. It particularly relies on Lijphart's analysis of the political system of the Netherlands. However, as has been rightly noted by Hanspeter Kriesi, the consociational type of democracy 'is today no longer applicable to any political system' (Kriesi 1998, 357; Marin 1987). This is perhaps one reason why Lijphart moved on to his conception of two models of democracy, of which the consensus model is most similar to the consociational type but with somewhat broader definitional criteria. Lijphart himself says that all consociational democracies can be labelled as consensual, but the reverse does not apply. This may also explain (and to a certain extent perhaps also justify) Lijphart's abandoning the use of the more precise term 'segmentation' in his newer conception of two models of democracy and his replacing it with more common expressions like 'social and cultural heterogeneity'. Sartori is right, however, that Lijphart's term 'plural societies' is not only overly broad but above all is misleading and suggests something qualitatively positive (Sartori 1994, 70).

REPRESENTATIVENESS, EFFICIENCY AND EFFECTIVENESS

As Sartori says, whereas the English (Westminster) type of democracy sacrifices the representativeness of parliament in favour of 'efficient government', the European 'continental'[6] type of democracy sacrifices the political efficiency of government to the representativeness of parliament (Sartori 1968b, 469; 1994, 53). Sartori notes in this regard that in some countries a more satisfactory equilibrium can be found between the government's ability to act and the parliament's representativeness (for example, in countries where there is an 'impure' system of proportional representation and at the same time only a relatively small number of political parties). Finally, Sartori stresses,

Nonetheless, from the view-point of institutional engineering the fact remains that we cannot build a representational system that maximizes at one and the same time the function of functioning and the function of mirroring. (Sartori 1968b, 469; 1994, 53)

On the contrary, Liam Anderson writes,

Indeed, it is consensus systems rather than majoritarian systems that involve a sacrifice in representativeness for greater effectiveness. (Anderson 1999, 27)

Anderson investigated the data Lijphart presented in his 1999 book *Patterns of Democracy* and arrived at two interesting conclusions:

Consensus democracy is inherently prescriptive as a model of constitutional design in that advocates invariably accompany the presentation of favorable results with a discussion of 'lessons' and 'recommendations' for newly democratizing countries. Such recommendations inevitably stress the importance of adopting a PR [proportional representation] based electoral system and the benefits of multiparty coalition governments. The results presented here indicate that in the sphere of macroeconomic policy, these [core] features of consensus democracy are associated with *unfavorable* outcomes. (Anderson 1999, 15)

It appears that

the superior performance of consensus democracy with respect to macroeconomic outcomes is primarily attributable to corporatism in the case of unemployment, and both corporatism and central bank independence in the case of inflation. (Anderson 1999, 14)[7]

Moreover, it is exactly those features (neocorporatism and an independent central bank) which according to Anderson explain the good socioeconomic results of consensus democracy that have nothing in common with democratic representativeness (Anderson 2001, 430).

Therefore, according to Anderson, it is not majoritarian but consensus democracies that sacrifice representativeness in favour of greater effectiveness. Was Sartori then wrong when he said that it is the Westminster democracies (or majoritarian democracies, in Lijphart's terminology) that sacrifice representativeness of parliament for greater efficiency? Not at all. In my opinion, it is necessary to distinguish between two different meanings of the words efficiency and effectiveness: 1) efficiency in the sense of political decisiveness (the ability to make decisions quickly)—the sense in which the word was used by, among others, Maurice Duverger (1988), Raymond Aron (1960a, 11–42), and Matthew S. Shugart and John M. Carey (1992), as well as Giovanni Sartori, of course; and 2) effectiveness in terms of socioeconomic outcomes or performance—the sense in which that word was used by, for example, Arend Lijphart and Liam Anderson.

In my opinion, here lies the apparent contradiction between Sartori and Anderson. The terms *efficiency/effectiveness* are not always used by political scientists in the same sense. The matter is even more complicated because no relationship necessarily exists between the two basic meanings of the words *efficiency/effectiveness*.

A government can be politically efficient and yet achieve unsatisfactory socioeconomic results. Conversely, a politically inefficient government (that is lacking in action capacity) can nevertheless achieve economic or other kinds of success (Novák 1996). In the past, when a country was politically efficient, like Great Britain, it did not necessarily achieve outstanding socioeconomic performances. This was noted by Raymond Aron (1965, 159, 165–66), who observed that a country whose political institutions function well can still make errors in economic policy that are more serious than those of countries whose political institutions do not function as well.

Duverger, Sartori, Shugart, Carey and, later, Kaiser, Lehnert, Miller and Sieberer (2002, 313–31)[8] describe a tradeoff between the representativeness of parliament and the decisiveness (efficiency) of government. Lijphart in contrast argues that this tradeoff does not exist because the consensus model of democracy is better not only in terms of the representativeness of parliament but also at least as good in terms of effectiveness. He understands effectiveness in the sense of socioeconomic performances, however.

Moreover, effectiveness in the sense of socioeconomic performances need not be related to the representativeness of a parliament, as Lijphart believes, but rather to legitimacy of the political system, as was long ago explained by Seymour Martin Lipset (1959, 86; 1960; 1994).[9] In that case there is no tradeoff between socioeconomic effectiveness and legitimacy. This is because greater legitimacy need not be accompanied by decreased effectiveness. Rather, there can exist all combinations of the two so that a high level of legitimacy can be accompanied by either high or low socioeconomic effectiveness, and so can a low level of legitimacy. On the other hand, efficiency in the sense of political decisiveness

> is closely related to identifiability—the ability of voters to identify the choices of competing potential governments that are being represented to them in electoral campaigns. (Shugart and Carey 1992, 8–9)[10]

In any case it is true that the idea of a tradeoff between the representativeness of parliament and efficiency—in the sense of the political decisiveness of the government—continues to be valid, and both (representativeness and decisiveness) cannot be maximised at the same time. One must be privileged at the expense of the other or an effort must be made to achieve a fair balance between them. That equilibrium, according to Sartori, can result from the combination of an impure proportional electoral system and a party system having a relatively limited number of political parties; that is, moderate pluralism. Just such a relative equilibrium is favoured by the German political scientists André Kaiser, Matthias Lehnert, Bernhard Miller and Ulrich Sieberer (2002, 329), who adjudge that the 'optimal tradeoff' between the two models of democracy is a middle path represented by the 'minimal winning coalition'. The pluralitarian[11] model, according to them, is characterised by single-party government representing only a relative majority (or put otherwise, the largest minority[12]). The ultimate consensus model would be an 'all-party regime' in the Swiss mode. In brief, a putative middle, mixed or optimal solution would be majoritarian in that the government represents the absolute majority of individual preferences, but no more than necessary.

Kaiser and his colleagues are right that when evaluating the qualities of a democracy[13] it is not necessary to prioritise representativeness (they give preference to the terms 'inclusion of preferences' and 'inclusiveness') simply and absolutely, but it is also necessary to take into account the dimension of responsibility (or efficiency in the sense of the political decisiveness of a government). I believe, however, that even this 'middle' or 'balanced' solution cannot be mechanistically recommended without taking into account the particular circumstances that pertain. Under certain conditions we can upset the balance in one direction or the other. For example, in a country riven by ethnic, religious or language cleavages, it is possible to give a bit more priority to the representativeness of the parliament at the expense of the decisiveness of the government. On the other hand, in a country that is relatively homogeneous culturally it is better to prioritise governmental decisiveness to a certain extent at the expense of the representativeness of parliament. This point, in my opinion, should play a key role in any discussion of Lijphart's consensus model.

IS THE CONSENSUS MODEL OF DEMOCRACY BETTER FOR ALL COUNTRIES?

Aristotle (1932, 289) in his *Politics* thoroughly developed the idea that it is not a question of which political regime, form of government or constitution is the 'absolute best' but also—in fact, mainly—which political regime is best under the given circumstances. According to Aristotle, if indeed there is some absolutely best form of government, it only makes sense to strive for it when no external obstacles prevent it—that is, only under exceptionally favourable circumstances, which almost never occur. Under ordinary circumstances, we must try to arrive at a form of government suitable to the given conditions.

In contrast, Lijphart has tried more and more since the 1990s to promote the consensus model as 'better' than the majoritarian model *for all democracies*. He urges newly democratising countries especially to decide in favour of the consensus model. Lijphart in his latest publications is slipping even more into the 'pre-Aristotelian' approach. He compares the two models as if it matters which of them can be proposed as the best for all countries that opt for democracy:

> These conclusions have an extremely important practical implication: because the overall performance record of the consensus democracies is clearly superior to that of the majoritarian democracies, the consensus option is the more attractive choice for countries designing their first democratic constitutions or contemplating democratic reform. This recommendation is particularly pertinent, and even urgent, for societies that have deep cultural and ethnic cleavages, *but it is also relevant for more homogeneous countries.* (Lijphart 1999, 301–2)

Lijphart expressed this belief even more unequivocally in his famous discussion with Rudy B. Andeweg:

> Consensus democracy is the preferable form of democracy for all countries, including those that are largely homogeneous. (Lijphart 2001b, 131)

I believe that we should approach things differently. We should pose the question: Under what conditions does the consensus model work best? Or more precisely, in what circumstances do we basically have no choice because the consensus model is to all intents and purposes the only realistic possibility to sustain democracy? Such is the case, it seems to me, in a country that is divided on linguistic or religious lines, like Belgium. In such cases one can agree with what Raymond Aron (1965, 231) has written that when a country is too far divided by the question of what the best regime is or what needs to be done in a particular situation, it is often better to settle for partial paralysis. In such cases the majoritarian model is not appropriate.

We should also consider the type of country where it is possible to implement, without major damage, the majoritarian model, and specifically its fundamental element, the majoritarian electoral system (or the more generally electoral system with majoritarian effect). In such countries, where a relative homogeneous culture and small ideological distance between the relevant political parties allow implementation of the majoritarian model, we can ask whether the consensus model might nevertheless be more suitable. We would not always be able to do what Lijphart does, which is to apply the same criteria for evaluation in every such country, or at least to give the same weight to each evaluative criterion. Comparisons among countries with more or less divergent models would have to be approached differently.[14] A criterion, which is important or even compelling and imperative in a country that is culturally very heterogeneous, can nearly be without importance in a country whose culture is relatively homogeneous (and vice versa). Therefore it is not possible to mechanically 'count up points' for or against 'representativeness' when it is a matter of life and death for one country and for another is much less important.

Robert Dahl, among others, explains how we should proceed:

> Whether people committed to the democratic process find it reasonable to adopt majority rule for all collective decisions, impose limits on majority rule, or move toward consensual arrangements therefore depends in part on the conditions under which they expect collective decisions will be made. If and when these conditions change, arrangements judged suitable in previous circumstances may be modified in one direction or another—toward stricter majoritarianism or toward greater nonmajoritarianism. (Dahl 1989, 161)

Thus, we arrive at this concise statement by Sartori:

> Along a continuum whose polar ends are 'always majoritarianism' or 'never majoritarianism', the concrete democracies are likely to be all the more majoritarian the more they are consensual, homogeneous (culturally), and non-segmented (in their structure of cleavages), and all the less majoritarian (i.e., consociational) the less these characteristics obtain. Somewhat differently restated, while we always find a blend of majoritarian and non-majoritarian decisions, the proportions vary, and vary in response to this rule of thumb: the greater the presence of intense minorities, the less zero-sum governing is advisable and democratically feasible. (Sartorti 1987, 240)[15]

I would add this to what Sartori says: unfortunately, in practice the correct prescriptions as laid out by Sartori and Dahl are not implemented. For example, in countries where it would be best to emphasise the majoritarian element, we can find that they are not sufficiently strengthened.

CONCLUSION

Giovanni Sartori rightly rejects the influential later opinions of Arend Lijphart, who holds that the consensus model is best for all democratic countries. He notes with reason that the concepts employed by Lijphart in his grand general theory of two models of democracy subtly suggest the superiority of consensus democracies over majoritarian ones. In my opinion, a problem exists in Lijphart's general theory. This problem results from the commingling of two concepts: efficiency in the sense of governmental decisiveness and effectiveness in the sense of socioeconomic performances. Lijphart's thesis is based directly on the confusion of those two different concepts. It apparently follows that the existence of a tradeoff between the representativeness of a parliament and the efficiency of a government is only the 'conventional wisdom', which Lijphart seeks to overturn and thereby lead a 'theoretical revolution' as conceived by Thomas Kuhn.

It is necessary to side with Sartori against Lijphart and underscore that the tradeoff between representativeness and efficiency in the sense of governmental decisiveness unquestionably still exists. It is not possible to maximise the representativeness of parliament and governmental efficiency at the same time. One must either decide to give preference to one at the expense of the other or try to achieve a reasonable equilibrium between the two—in which case neither is maximised, of course. To make the choice, it is necessary above all to take into account existing circumstances and not offer one and only one model of democracy to all kinds of societies. That is exactly the 'pre-Aristotelian' approach.

Sartori is also correct when he writes that consensus (and even more so consociational) institutions and elements (such as the minority veto) may engender more consensus breaking than consensus making (Sartori 1994, 72). This was demonstrated in the case of the collapse of the Czechoslovak federation, which in 1992 Lijphart considered to be one example of consociational democracy. Insofar as countries that are culturally homogeneous are concerned, Rudy B. Andeweg (2001) persuasively established that unthinkingly promoting consensus (or even consociational) institutions could in some countries contribute to the advance of extreme political parties, just as we have witnessed in the past few decades.

At the time, in the late 1960s, Lijphat's old theory of four types of democracy provided a useful contribution to the development of empirically based theories of democracy, as Sartori, among others, recognised. However, segmentation, as a key conceptual element of the consociational type of democracy, was significantly weakened at the end of the 1960s, if not entirely dismantled. This allows us to understand why Lijphart's later concept of consensus democracy attempted to distance itself from segmentation, but the consensus model of democracy is not better overall than the Westminster model. 'Consensus' institutions, moreover, do not necessarily lead to consensus. They often lead to very long, sometimes even year-long efforts to form a government, which then fall apart only a few months later.

Lijphart's conviction was that the basic elements of consensus democracy, including the party system, the electoral system and the kind of government, which favours the representativeness of parliament over governmental decisiveness, are associated with slightly better socioeconomic outcomes. In contradiction, however, Anderson's, Lane's and Ersson's calculations indicate worse socioeconomic performances. Better socioeconomic outcomes are associated with neocorporatism and an independent central bank, according to Anderson. However, both neocorporatism and the independence of the central bank have logic that is very different from the central institutional elements that Lijphart generally prefers, such as the proportional electoral system, broad multiparty systems, oversized coalition governments and so forth. Not only the independence of the central bank but also neocorporatism is not necessarily linked to 'consensual' institutions, as Lane and Ersson rightly explain. They contend also that no correlation exists between neocorporatism and better socioeconomic results *in highly developed countries* (Lane and Ersson 2000, 240–43). Ferdinand Müller-Rommel (2008) concluded the same, adding that the better economic and social outcomes of consensus democracy can be explained more by the fact that there are more less-developed countries among the majoritarian democracies than by greater socioeconomic effectiveness of the institutions of consensus democracy.

Lijphart's (2001b, 131) thesis that consensus democracy is more suitable than the Westminster model for all democratic countries is unsustainable. One of the main reasons it still has a number of supporters is that it seemingly offers a simple recipe for success in practically all circumstances in all democratic countries—and not only in those that are ethnically, linguistically or religiously heterogeneous. Institute this or that institution in every country and it will 'be better'. It won't. We would do better to try to choose those institutions that are suitable for the given circumstances, as was suggested by Aristotle in his day. That is much more burdensome and difficult. It is not enough to mechanically apply this or that template to every democratic country. Finally, as Sartori and Sani have shown, the 'consociational democracy' which has a proportional representation electoral system is not capable of resolving the problems of a polarised society.

NOTES

1. For my earlier critical analysis of Lijphart, see namely Novák 1997a (2000). I wrote about Sartori's critique of Lijphart in 2004 (Novák 2004).

2. This does not mean, however, that Lijphart's earlier typology of democracy (consociational, depoliticised, centripetal and centrifugal) was entirely without problems, even if it was generally accepted. Among its critics we can cite, for example, Bogaards 2000, 395–423; Halpern 1986, 181–97; Horowitz 1991; and Schedelen 1984, 19–55. Lijphart (2002, 11–22) answered his critics in a special issue of the journal *Acta Politica*.

3. Duverger as 'centrism' often described this form of government, which Lijphart termed 'consensus'. By this he meant 'governing *by* the centre', which is the antithesis of 'governing *at* the centre'. The latter, according to Duverger, characterises Westminster democracy. He contends there exists a so-called paradox of the centre in which the centre governs only when it does not exist (Duverger 1988, 191). 'Government by the centre' roughly corresponds to what Lijphart termed the 'consociational type' of democracy, a wide coalition encompassing all 'segments', or something like an 'oversized coalition' or 'surplus majority coalition' within the framework of Lijphart's consensus model. On the other hand, 'governing at the centre' is normal in Westminster democracy whether it is the left or the right that governs. The logic of the institution requires governing near the centre.

4. The Czechoslovak constitution, inherited from the former communist regime, led the new situation of the postcommunist regime into a blind alley because thirty-one federal depu-

ties (out of 350) were enough to block any constitutional change. Therefore the breakup of the federation was essentially 'programmed' in advance. In part, the Czechoslovak federation was broken up in order to unblock the political system at a time when the country was undergoing radical transformation and it was necessary to carry out profound reforms (Vodička 2003; Novák 1997b).

5. 'Pluralism' is one of those concepts that were for Sartori the most frequently and inappropriately 'stretched'. He therefore devoted great efforts to define the term as clearly as possible (Sartori 1997d; 2000b).

6. In some of his texts, Sartori spoke of the 'French' type of democracy in this regard. This, however, applied only to the French Third and Fourth Republics and not to today's Fifth Republic. Moreover, the 'continental' European type does not describe all the democratic regimes on the European continent, where we find other political regimes that are rather closer to majoritarian on the continuum between 'consensus' and 'majoritarian' democracies. In the first rank among these is the French Fifth Republic, which has a semi-presidential regime (Duverger 1988, 108–9).

7. Richard Rose also compared the economic efficiency of democracies that have a majoritarian electoral system with that of democracies that have a system of proportional representation (the latter of which he described as 'representational'). He allowed that 'there is no consistent link between electoral system and economic performance' (Rose 1992, 17).

8. These authors give preference to the term 'responsibility'.

9. Nothing prevents us from determining, like Raymond Aron, for example, that a well-functioning democracy requires both adequate parliamentary representativeness and effectiveness in the sense of socioeconomic performances. Such a statement does not imply a tradeoff between them.

10. Efficiency in the sense of political decisiveness is sometimes identified as accountability, sanctionability, legislative governability or simply responsibility (Birch 1964; Kaiser et al. 2002).

11. The word *pluralitarian* is derived from the electoral system known in English as 'single-member plurality' or as 'first-past-the-post'.

12. In exceptional cases, this need not even be the largest minority. It has happened a few times in Great Britain that the party that won the most votes did not get the most seats in Parliament. This also happened in 1953 in Austria under a proportional electoral system: the Austrian People's Party (ÖVP) won one mandate more than the Social Democratic Party (SPÖ), even though a marginally greater percent of the electorate voted for the latter party (74 mandates with 41.3 percent of the total vote for the ÖVP, but only 73 mandates with 42.1 percent of the total vote for the SPÖ).

13. Leonardo Morlino observes that the measure of a democracy cannot be reduced only to its responsiveness to the attitudes of its citizens; its electoral responsibility must also be taken into account. In that respect Morlino is close to Sartori. In his important essay, he quotes Sartori with regard to the connection between responsibility and responsiveness (Morlino 2009, 220).

14. The concepts of majoritarian and consensus democracies are only ideal types in the sense of Max Weber, which actual political systems can only more or less approximate.

15. Renske Doorenspleet and Huib Pellikaan (2013) state that a decision in favour of centralisation or decentralisation need not be the same for all kinds of societies: while centralisation is suitable for homogeneous societies, decentralisation is best for heterogeneous societies. This is not a revolutionary discovery, but with regard to Lijphart's later conception, neither is it without usefulness.

Chapter Eight

Giovanni Sartori as a Political Theorist

On His Polemics with Marxism

Marek Bankowicz

Giovanni Sartori, the eminent Italian scholar to whom this volume is devoted, made his mark especially as the author of groundbreaking studies within comparative politics, which have set the course in political science for decades. Sartori, however, also intensively studied political theory, and the preceding chapter picks up on his theory of democracy. From early on, Sartori also immersed himself in philosophy and political philosophy, especially in the works of Croce, Hegel, Kant and Marx. Unfortunately, many of Sartori's books on political philosophy are only little known and even less read: they were written early in his career and they have not been translated into English. Philosophy played a key role in Sartori's scholarship, as also shown in chapter 2. Political philosophy was his entry ticket to academia, and its close reading significantly influenced his later work. Hence, as I argue, any discussion on Sartori would be incomplete without referencing his work on political theory.

If Sartori's contributions to comparative politics have been covered by many (in here and elsewhere), the aim here is to show Sartori as a political philosopher. I will do so by turning to the probably least-known works of his in this regard—on Marxism. We need to understand that Sartori was an authority on and critique of Marxism, even though, as we know, Marx's thought intrigued him and drew his attention from the very beginning of his career. Furthermore, throughout his prolific life, Sartori frequently returned to the topic of Marxism. Soon after the collapse of the global communist system, Sartori wrote,

> I simply contend that Marxism has been by far the most forceful and pervasive ideology of our time, and thus the end of the ideology of Marxism signifies the end of an ideology that has actually permeated our thinking and conditioned our life experience—in short, the end of ideology as we know it. (Sartori 1991c, 438)

This chapter offers Sartori's take on Marx, often critical and polemical in nature. It is structured as follows. First, I focus on Sartori's consistent distinction between Marx as a philosopher and Marx as an ideologist, following which I zoom in on Sartori's reading of Marx's (and Hegel's) dialectics. In the next section, I revisit Sartori's examination of the political aspects of Marx's ideology, such as democracy, revolution and the concept of the dictatorship of the proletariat. In the last part, I briefly introduce Sartori's views on the relationship between Marxism and Leninism.

'YOUNG' MARX VERSUS 'MATURE' MARX— FROM PHILOSOPHY TO IDEOLOGY

In 1951, Sartori published *Da Hegel a Marx: La dissoluzione della filosofia hegeliana*,[1] the leitmotif of which is the study of the connections and relationships between Hegelianism and Marxism. Sartori strongly juxtaposed the 'young' Marx and the 'mature' Marx and indirectly demonstrated the overall inconsistencies in Marxism. However, Sartori did not percieve the 'mature' Marx in a positive light. Quite the contrary—for Sartori, the philosophy of the 'mature' Marx was regressive compared to the ideas of the 'young' Marx. The 'young' Marx was an interesting philosopher and a dynamic researcher of the human condition as well as a person who searched for the truth and who had broad horizons of thoughts that earned him recognition and respect. Conversely, wrote Sartori, the 'mature' Marx was

> the Marx of 'historical materialism' and Marx the 'economist', who renounced his 'philosophical awareness'. (Sartori 1951, 219)

Consequently, Marx passed on from fascinating, creative philosophical deliberation to a more or less ossified search for a 'systematic theory', as Sartori (1951, 221) called it. That theory's allegedly scientific framework is provided by historical materialism and economics, that is, a tendency to see the essence of all phenomena in economic terms. Historical materialism has become a canon, a fossilised and unshakable formula, which Marx announced once and for all as absolute scientific truth. Gianfranco Pasquino, one of the contributors to this volume, has observed as follows:

> As for Marxism, Sartori rejects it because, on the one hand, it does not constitute a falsifiable theory, according to the criteria suggested by Popper, and, on

the other, it fails to give any appreciable space to political factors; worse, it does not recognise the autonomy of politics. (Pasquino 2009, 170)

This state of affairs results in numerous negative consequences, probably the most important of which is a total disregard for the human being as the subject of history. According to Sartori,

> For Marx, who gives economic and scientific attributes to historical materialism, reference to the human being as an 'active force' in history is omitted rather than left for guessing, if a human being is a society and a society is history with rights and economic structures. (Sartori 1951, 235)

Characteristically, when Marx mentions topics that concern human beings, he is interested in the human being only in a general sense, as a species or a type. He almost never refers to a specific human being at all. As Sartori put it,

> When Marx says, 'a person' or 'people', he says 'historical species', or 'social species', which is not a naturalistic and physiological species, but, to the same extent, is a 'species' in its uniformist lack of individuality among specimens which accompany it. An individual is never perceived by Marx as a 'subject', but as an 'object'. (Sartori 1951, 268)

Marx is hostile to the individualistic idea of the human being. According to Sartori (1997c, 67), the individual is a total abstraction to Marx. Marx's anthropology is an extreme example of social anthropology. From his perspective, the liberation of a human being coincides with the disintegration of the individual, that is, 'the supreme freedom is supreme community-orientation' (Sartori 1951, 289).

TRAPS OF DIALECTICS

The 'economicisation' assumed by Marx covers everything without exception, including the dialectics inherited from Hegel, which Marx 'materialises' and dresses in the robes of

> the ontological and structural demiurge of reality. Whereas the essence, the vital juice of dialectics is, according to Marx, contained in the perpetuity of 'movement' and in 'negation-destruction'. (Sartori 1951, 237)

In its materialistic form, dialectics ceased to be a type of mediation among various ideas, concepts, thoughts and solutions. A materialist movement that manifests itself with negation-destruction is not able to create any actual synthesis, any new, higher quality. It can only result in the total destruction of the current state of affairs:

> In fact, Marx's dialectics exceed the scope of dialectics: it has retained its name but lost the essence. (Sartori 1951, 239)

What is more, Sartori proved that dialectics, in order to mean anything and still retain basic sense, must in a way assume an indeterminate relationship between its subjects and therefore stands in contradiction to determinism (Sartori 1951, 246). Consequently, reality and human history develop either dialectically or deterministically. Marxism falls prey to this obvious contradiction.

Criticism of ideology as false awareness leads Marx to, among other things, renounce ethics, which he treats as one form of bourgeois ideology and a type of mystification. In his opinion, the real purpose of ethics is to camouflage the genuine nature of capitalist society. The proletariat is free of false awareness and therefore does not need ethics or morality. Consequently, communist society, being classless, will not need ethics either (Sartori 1997c, 65):

> In line with this idea, Marx—addressing the proletariat—never propagates a moral crusade and does not encourage the proletariat to rebellion in the name of ethical re-vindication. (Sartori 1951, 260)

Meanwhile, clearly in contradiction of these assumptions, Marx's *Capital* is overloaded with ethical criticism of capitalism (Marx 2011).

As Sartori pointed out, Marxist discourse about capitalism in general is a sort of demonology that depicts capitalism as the embodiment of absolute evil in all possible fields and in all possible forms. The fight against capitalism, fuelled by boundless fanaticism, leads Marxism to the utopian constructs that in turn sustain its radical rejection of Western civility. This fight impoverishes communist ideology intellectually because exposing the absolute evil of capitalism is very often carried out by means of 'epithet-thinking'—as Sartori (1991c, 439–440) rightly termed it—which drives out and disregards thinking based on facts and reason.

The fact that Marx derives politics from philosophy is dangerous because it leads to the instrumentalisation of philosophical reflection and exposes it to pressure from current objectives of political activity. Philosophy aligned with politics and marked by clear political influences, that is, political philosophy, is always an aberration. This aberration deepens even further when such philosophy does not stop at theorising but clearly demonstrates what Sartori calls 'materialistic' ambitions, that is, when it not only desires to describe the world but also to serve as an important element in its reconstruction. At the same time, it does not confine itself to influencing the human mind but becomes the banner of political movements or parties striving for power, which Marx believes is its most important duty in the end. In that situation, however, we are always dealing with politics, not philosophy (Sartori 1951, 367). To put it differently, philosophy always loses out to politics.

What is, however, most visible in the case of Marx, according to Sartori, is his constant battle with Hegel, waged on all possible fields, in various ways and with different weapons. It could therefore seem that Hegel and Marx have diametrically opposed philosophical views. It turns out, however, that that is only an appearance of things. 'What is the relationship between Marx and Hegel?', Sartori asked and answered his own question in the following way:

> The relationship is as follows: Marx rebels against Hegel in terms of criticism of Hegel's 'conclusions' which are based on Hegelian 'foundations'; Marx rebels against Hegel, at the same time looking at Hegel. (Sartori 1951, 361–62)

Marx was a thinker who borrowed nearly all of his philosophical problems, his assumptions about philosophical reflection and his research tools from Hegel. He looks at the world from the Hegelian perspective and analyses it in the Hegelian way. His approach is not undermined by his engagement in polemics and disputes with Hegel, which is only a kind of mannerism.

AGAINST POLITICAL DEMOCRACY

In Sartori's (1987) famous book titled *The Theory of Democracy Revisited*, however, it was obviously not Marx's philosophy and its political implications that were the author's main object of interest. Nevertheless, it was here that Sartori extended on and, at the same time, sharpened his criticism of Marxism. He concluded that what is extremely important for understanding the nature of Marxism is to become aware of the fact that Marxism implies a radical negation of autonomy in politics. This results from Marx's extremely materialistic perception of history, according to which the history of humankind is largely determined by economic factors. Thus, politics as a phenomenon of social reality is deprived of larger significance and relegated to secondary rank. The worth of political democracy is negated by equating it with the capitalist system. Additionally, in Marxism, democracy is a form of class rule. Sartori wrote,

> From the point of view of Marxists, political democracy has no value in its own right, no inherent reason to exist, and is only a tool which enables those who exploit to dominate those who are exploited. To be more specific, politi-

cal democracy is the superstructure of capitalist and bourgeois oppression, and, consequently, may be reduced to capitalist democracy. (1987, 25)

By permanently aligning it with capitalism, Marx makes political democracy redundant in the communist system. There is no need to develop a model of noncapitalist political democracy. Instead one could say that economic democracy will appear as the only pure and true form of democracy. Consequently, economic democracy is tantamount to communist democracy—a slogan frequently used by Marx, mainly as a political weapon. Communist democracy was expected to be of an extra-political nature because it would only appear after 'crushing the state' ('crushing' is one of Marx's favourite words). In this sense there are no points of agreement between communist democracy and democracy tout court. By abolishing private property, communism will establish a new economic system in which the political system will ultimately prove to be completely redundant because the problem of power will be solved. Sartori (1987, 432) concluded that 'consequently, economic "democracy" comes down to communist "economy"'. In other words, a proper democracy, that is, a communist democracy, is an economy that has been organised and operates in line with the guidelines formulated by Marx.

By repudiating political democracy, Marxism undermines the principles of political and legal equality. It considers them to be mere formalities and—as Sartori (1987, 432) pointed out—'the term form is meant to be synonymous with appearance (delusion or deception)'. Sartori decisively rejected this line of reasoning. He treats political and legal equality, as well as equality of access to political power, as formal equalities only in a technical sense. The fact that these equalities are of a formal nature does not necessarily mean that they are hollow imitations of true equality or that they do not provide any protection to people against abuses of privilege, injustices and inequalities they encounter. 'What is formal is the method, not the result' (Sartori 1987, 433).

The force that drives Marxism to fight to change the face of the world is not a desire to ensure political and legal equality because it recognises those values as fictitious. Rather, it is the demand for economic equality—the only genuine equality—because that is the kind of equality that is a precondition for the grand process of liberating humankind. However, it must be strongly emphasised that economic equality itself is not the primary value esteemed by Marx. The most important value in Marxism is freedom, according to Sartori. As will be discussed later in this chapter, freedom is understood by Marxists completely differently than it is in the system of liberal democracy. Economic inequality is definitely a very important social problem, and opposition to injustice may be the cause of and justification for various laudable actions. Nevertheless, Sartori (1987, 422) doubted whether 'Marx taught us how to treat the illness of economic inequality'. Sartori concluded that the solution proposed by Marx resembles the old—and, in his opinion, primitive—egalitarian treatment recommended by Plato and others, which was convincingly criticised by Aristotle. Its essence is the use of state power to conduct a far-reaching reconstruction of society. The state's strength must be used against its former owners. For this reason, during the period of revolutionary transformation, the state, being a necessary evil, will be kept alive and will start to die only later. This differentiates Marxism from anarchism, which is always and everywhere hostile to the state. Still, the active use of state power during the revolutionary period is to some extent at odds with Marxist canons of historical materialism.

Sartori heavily criticised the excitement about a 'culture of revolution' promoted by Marxism. Marxists believe that the world can be changed only by means of revolution and that violence used for the right cause is not only fully justified, it is in fact laudable. This is a very dangerous strategy because, as Sartori (1991c, 439) warned, one needs to remember that 'collective violence simply destroys'.

According to Sartori, the concept of the dictatorship of the proletariat, considered by Marx as a period of revolutionary transformation of capitalist society into a communist one, did not require resort to dictatorship. However, those who elaborated on Marx's doctrine, such as Lenin, considered that an absolute necessity:

> The Marxist dictatorship of the proletariat was not expected to consist of establishing a state dictatorship but destroying the state by means of the proletariat as the dictator. To Marx, dictatorship means the same as revolution, i.e. the 'use of force'. (Sartori 1987, 564)

The concept of the proletariat as collective dictator seems very risky, and if we assume that Sartori's view is correct, we would probably have to relegate it to the company of other utopian ideas. Sartori had no illusion whatsoever that Marx, when he outlined the assumptions and aims of the dictatorship of the proletariat, was only using a metaphor or figure of speech. It was nothing of the kind—Marx meant resorting, should the need arise, to violence on such a wide scale that the dictatorship of the proletariat would inevitably become a rule of terror exercised by the 'army of the proletariat'; that is, an armed proletariat. However, it should be reiterated that Marx believed this scenario was only one of the possible paths to communism.

Sartori believed that the creator of Marxism had a serious problem in his conception of both capitalist and revolutionary rule and that, generally speaking, he completely misunderstood power as a political phenomenon. In his fascination with the ownership of property, Marx understood power as a substantial value, that is, as a type of property, which one can hold just like any other material asset. Consequently, he completely neglected the relational and functional natures of power, focusing only on power as a form of class-based economic rule that gives rise to political power. He made a huge mistake by confusing one source of power with power itself (Sartori 1987, 423).

COMMUNISM AS A 'HEAVENLY CITY'

According to Sartori, the Marxist ideal of a well-ordered society, that is, communism, is quite naive. Marx believed that not only private property, which results in one person exploiting the other, but also the division of labour, which enslaves human beings, will be done away with. Sartori said that scholars of Marxism pay insufficient attention to this. If it is Marxian absolute freedom that will liquidate human alienation once and for all, then paradoxically 'the ideal (communist) society is the most extreme example of a pure and simple libertarian society' (Sartori 1987, 533). Marx's 'disarming libertarian sincerity' is evident when he and Engels try to predict the specific indications and features of the perfect world of the future in *The Communist Manifesto* (Marx and Engels 2014). Communism was expected to bring about a stateless, self-governed, harmonious community of the people living in conditions of economic abundance, following the rules of direct democracy (Sartori 2005a, 227).

This vision of communism has a striking resemblance to anarchist ideals, which Marx, in fact, always fiercely opposed for their utopian nature (Sartori 1951, 285). Marx posited that liberation from all economic limitations and necessity would result in a state of total freedom. It is very difficult, however, not to get the impression that human freedom can only be attained by some act of liberation that is almost metaphysical (Sartori 1951, 291).[2] In the end, Sartori (1987, 558–59) wrote, we are simply left with a 'heavenly city'.

Disregarding the extreme utopianism, which is evident in such a completely unrealistic vision, Sartori contended that Marx's ideal society was, after all, expected to be created on the basis of fulfilment of the idea of freedom. The Marxian ideal was only coincidentally the fulfilment of the ideal of equality, which to Marx was a complementary and secondary value. Communism was conceived both as the crowning achievement and the completion of the process of liberating humanity, rather than as the triumph of egalitarianism:

> Marx's message of salvation was libertarian and not egalitarian in its nature. Marx put forward a counter-ideal which was a libertarian ideal in its most extreme and millennial form. (Sartori 1987, 559)

Consequently, Sartori did not treat Marxism as an ideology of equality but as an ideology of freedom, although misunderstood and wrongly implemented. At the same time, it is an ideology searching for some formula of alternative democracy, placing itself in strong opposition to traditional democracy, which—according to Sartori—must always be liberal democracy. The longing for an alternative democracy, as well as the drafting of a vision of a society of the future, culminates and at the same time ennobles the whole history of humankind by pointing the way to a final triumph of freedom. This is the crucial connection between the political philosophies of Marx and Rousseau, who was the great predecessor of Marx. Rousseau may be the patron of those who strive for liberal democracy, but Marx is the inspiration for those who want to negate it completely (Sartori 1993, 242).

What raises doubt in Sartori's mind is the communist model of 'popular democracy' or 'proletarian democracy' advocated by Marxists. After all, Marx was not brave enough to reject democracy as a whole, being aware of the risk that involves. He was particularly aware that democracy has since ancient times had positive connotations. For that reason, as we have said, he looked for some 'different', alternative democracy. In that way Marxism has become one of the movements of so-called adjective democracy. 'Popular democracy' or 'proletarian democracy' may be shelved next to higher, genuine, organic, direct or national democracy. According to Sartori, all these other democracies have nothing to do with normal democracy and in fact are concealed dictatorships, ashamed to show their faces. Democracy either exists or it does not exist. There is no 'other democracy'. Sartori wrote,

> The so-called other democracies resemble the Egyptian Phoenix, which is mentioned in Metastasio's charming poem: *Che ci sia ognun lo dice, dove sia nessun lo sa.*[3] (Sartori 1987, 584)

In fact, the formulation 'popular democracy' is a logical error known as *idem per idem*—the same for the same. This is because democracy itself means the rule of the people. Consequently, popular democracy becomes popular rule by the people, as if nonpopular rule by the people was possible at all. Marxism seems to take such a position, which is absurd from a logical point of view.

LENIN'S 'BETRAYAL'

According to Sartori, Lenin 'betrayed' Marx, primarily as regards the relationship between the proletariat and the party. Lenin's concept of the party avant-garde, put forward in *What Is to Be Done?* (Lenin 1961), has no basis or justification in Marx's doctrine. For Lenin, the party, which gathers in aware and correctly thinking revolutionaries, repels and finally replaces the real proletariat. Sartori believed that Lenin changed the protagonist, the main carrier of the revolution. In Lenin's works the Marxist revolutionaries becomes the avant-garde 'above' the proletariat (Sartori 1987, 568).

Lenin decisively questioned the value of any democracy, which he considered to be equivalent to the state. From that position, every type of democracy is the organised and systematic use of force against the people. According to Sartori, when Lenin discussed the dictatorship of the proletariat, he surprisingly changed his tone and referred to democracy in a positive sense. He did not consider the proletariat to be a collective dictator, writing that the dictatorship of the proletariat means organising oneself in avant-gardes of oppressed masses in the ruling class in order to crush the oppressors (Bankowicz 1995, 98–101). At the same time, he said that 'this dictatorship will be democracy for the people' (Lenin 1972, 130). There was, however, no contradiction or change of tone in Lenin's philosophy, and therefore it is difficult to agree with Sartori. Lenin openly said that the dictatorship of the proletariat implies the use of force, and yet it is also democracy. In other words, the dictatorship of the proletariat is the state, only with the exception that it resorts to force not in the interest of the minority of those who exploit but the vast majority of those who are exploited, contrary to earlier political systems. One could argue that the dictatorship of the proletariat, which channels state violence in a different direction than before, is more democratic than 'other' democracies, including bourgeois democracy. The dictatorship of the proletariat can be understood to be fated to disappear, as it will not be necessary after the state is abolished, something which will take place once the stage of full communism has been achieved. In this respect, Lenin fully shared Marx's ideals.

The state constructed by Lenin in Russia proved to be a complete catastrophe. What still remains unclear is whether that state of affairs was the consequence of distortion of the doctrine or maybe only of its practical application. Let us quote Sartori once again:

> Lenin was spared the age of the omnipotent, raging police, which became the pillar of the state called, ironically, the Soviet Republic. It was, however, about to happen soon. Lenin brought Marx's heavenly city to earth, but it changed into hell here. (Sartori 1987, 572)

Sartori treated the bankruptcy of the global communist system in 1989 as tantamount to the end of Marxist ideology, but it did not mean to him the end of Marxism as a philosophy. He wrote,

> Marx will remain on our shelves as an author whom we discuss and quote, alongside other classics, but the 'revolutionary philosopher' that Marx launched into the path of history as the first real-world philosopher-king is dead and gone. (Sartori 1991c, 438)

CONCLUSION

Sartori's critical analysis of Marxism brings a very unique approach to the traditional polemics against that ideology. Even when he presents well-known anti-Marxist trains of thought, he does it in an attractive way. What are therefore the originalities in Sartori's perspective? Sartori thought that Marxism was the essence of ideology because the end of Marxism would be tantamount to the collapse of ideology as we know it. According to Sartori, the abstractionism of Marxism causes it to treat real human beings with contempt. For him, dialectics are inevitably connected with indeterminism, while Marxist deterministic ideology is absolutely erroneous in its logic. Sartori accuses Marxism of totally misunderstanding the phenomenon of political power, regarding it as an ordinary type of material property. However, the most impressive point of Sartori's thinking on Marxism is his opinion that Marxism is in its deepest heart not egalitarian but extremely libertarian. That, Sartori believed, is a consequence of the Marxist ideal of communism as universal happiness on Earth and the end of the long, bad history of class struggle and exploitation.

NOTES

1. The book is based on Giovanni Sartori's PhD dissertation.
2. Here Marx is a real disciple of Hegel. According to Marx, a man achieves full and unfettered freedom when he dissolves his individuality into a perfect communist society. Hegel claimed that such a state could be achieved only by entering into the realm of 'Absolute Spirit'.
3. Everybody says it exists, but nobody knows where.

Conclusion

Michal Kubát and Martin Mejstřík

Giovanni Sartori never wished to be confined in the ivory tower of the academic world. Besides his scientific engagement, it was both his wide interests and his particular character traits that predestined him to become a publicly active interpreter of political events. In all the manifold areas of his interests and activities there is a scarlet thread of combativeness. Sartori fought a number of battles, not all of which he won, with unusual tenacity. The individual chapters of this volume illustrate this point well.

As echoed also by Capoccia earlier on, Sartori unquestionably won his struggle to establish political science as a substantially new and independent field of study in postwar Italy. He founded the discipline both in terms of its prestige and as an institution. He educated a number of students who today rank among leading political scholars in Italy and worldwide (this includes Domenico Fisichella, Leonardo Morlino, Gianfranco Pasquino, a contributor to this volume, Stefano Passigli, Giuliano Urbani and many others). Sartori's influence on the discipline of political science is not limited to his native Italy. He achieved great renown in Latin America (interestingly, many of his texts were translated into Spanish rather than into English), as well as in Central Europe. After the fall of communism in 1989, Sartori's works played a key role in the process of renewal, or more accurately the building of political science in the latter region. This is because before 1989 political science did not exist at all in several Central European countries, such as Czechoslovakia, while in others, like Poland, although it certainly did exist, it functioned only in a very limited fashion. Thus Sartori 'co-founded' the field—at a distance—in many of the postcommunist countries. The fact that the majority of the authors in this volume come from Central Europe speaks for itself.

On the other hand, Sartori was less successful in his struggle with the methodology of comparative politics. Although Sartori presented his own comprehensive methodology of the social sciences, he was unable to break through the mainstream quantitative methodology that completely dominated the Anglo-Saxon world of comparative politics. That methodology was opposite in all ways to Sartori's concept of how research into political science should be done and the role comparative politics should play. That does not mean that Sartori's 'methodological voice' was not known and heard, but for the most part it did not reverberate.[1] Yet it is a paradox that contemporary political research rests on conceptual foundations that arose in the context of qualitative methodology as it was understood by Sartori. To a large extent his understanding was shared by all of the great generation of political scientists of the second half of the twentieth century, including the original behaviouralists headed by Robert A. Dahl (compare their statements in Daalder 1997 and Munck and Snyder 2007).

Contemporary political research is based on some specific concepts that were thought up by Sartori. In our volume, those are mainly represented by concepts from his theories of political parties and democratic regimes. That does not mean that those concepts are accepted without reservation or that they are properly applied. Sartori himself certainly doubted that when he observed some contemporary political analyses. The fact that in the study of parties and party systems it is simply impossible to ignore Sartori's minimalist definition of 'political party' or his typology of party systems is witness to his undoubted influence and importance. In that regard, Sartori's struggle for his own conceptual form of comparative political science was certainly successful.

Where Sartori was least successful was in his fight to shape the Italian politics of the 1990s. The transition from the 'first' to the 'second' Italian republic in that decade, and the various systemic reforms associated with it, all occurred in contradiction to what Sartori wanted and represented. He was unable to influence Italian politics very much. Was that, however, ever within his power? It appears that it was not within the power of any openly engaged political scientist who sought to institutionalise his own vision for the political system in that country without taking on a political office that provided a position of power.

Sartori's vision of the practical applicability of political science therefore remained stuck halfway. A political scientist can, and according to Sartori must, offer practical solutions to political problems, but how to put them into practice remains beyond his or her reach. Politicians decide that. The fact that many of them make poor decisions, to the detriment of things, is another matter. Academic political scientists cannot and do not have influence over that. A good example is Central Europe, in particular the recent case of the Czech Republic's 2012 introduction of direct presidential election. Politicians decided to abolish the traditional election of the president by Parliament and institute general, direct elections of the present. Nearly every Czech political scientist and constitutional lawyer vehemently warned against that reform. In vain. It is significant that many of the negative results of such a reform that the experts predicted eventually came to pass (Brunclík and Kubát 2019). Sartori was in the same situation in Italy in the 1990s. Everything he warned about occurred, without exception.

So Giovanni Sartori won some battles and lost others. He left us, however, an inheritance that has universal validity: political science has to be an applicable science, one that is useful in practice. Comparative politics has to offer a view of things that is generally comprehensible. It is a matter of explaining reality and pointing out advantages and disadvantages, especially the possible dangers of some solutions. Research in political science should not be too narrowly focused and specialised, without any practical impact, and should not be merely some kind of mental gymnastics.

The place of methodology in political science is related to that. What should be the main object of political research? The development of a method or answering questions? The two need not, of course, be separated. No one reasonable would doubt the need for methodology and the importance of its correct use in research. Methods, in the sense of research techniques, are surely important 'tools of political science', but they cannot substitute for research itself. They have to be useful aides to research. This was Sartori's point.

Contemporary political science is paradoxical. On the one hand, we see its rapid growth, while on the other it has taken a pause. We certainly know more, have more data, more sophisticated methods and techniques of research, but we are not producing as many theories and concepts as in the past. The problem, we would argue together with Sartori, lies in the quantification based on the cumulation of data. This, however, is only the start of the analysis and should not be its end. We must realise that contemporary political science is still relying on classic concepts from the second half of the twentieth century, many of which—as also shown throughout the volume—were put forward or influenced by Sartori. How did these classic concepts come about? Not in the gathering of a large amount of data and their sophisticated, quantitative manipulation. They arose on the basis of case studies and 'small-N' comparisons. Alfred Stepan expressed it well:

> But, if Linz had not been deeply immersed in the history and politics of Spain, would we have his fine-grained concept of 'authoritarianism'? What of Lijphart, Holland, and 'consociational democracy'? Sartori, Italy, and 'polarized pluralism'? Schmitter, Brazil, and 'societal corporatism'? Putnam, Italy, and 'social capital'? O'Donnell, Argentina, and 'bureaucratic authoritarianism'? Evans, Brazil, and 'triple alliance'? And it goes on. (Stepan 2007, 454)

Sartori was an empiricist, but of another, 'nonquantitative' kind. His empiricism was contextual. Political research should not ignore historical, cultural, religious, geographical and other contexts. Indeed, according to some, political science is a historical science per se (Schmitter 2007, 340). We can certainly have different views about that, but when we revisit Sartori's work (and that of the other 'classics' of world comparative politics), we see that they had wide-ranging knowledge that they consistently utilised—knowledge of history, philosophy, languages, literature and so on. This is what ultimately makes Sartori's work universal, inspiring and analytically useful, albeit challenging.

NOTE

1. At the very least, one can say that Sartori's methodology is known and employed beyond the discipline of comparative politics—for example, in the field of history (see Kubátová and Kubát 2018).

References

Alemann von, U. 2000. *Das Parteiensystem in der Bundesrepublik Deutschland*. Opladen: Leske and Budrich.
Almond, G. A. 1990. *A Discipline Divided: Schools and Sects in Political Science*. Newbury Park: Sage.
Almond, G. A., and J. S. Coleman, eds. 1960. *The Politics of the Developing Areas*. Princeton: Princeton University Press.
Amato, G., et al. 1991. 'Parlamentarismo e Presidenzialismo: Dibattito sulla Proposta di Giovanni Sartori'. *Il Politico* 56 (2): 201–55.
Anderson, L. 1999. 'The Implications of Institutional Design for Representative Democracy: Examining the Claims of Consensus Democracy'. Paper presented at APSA Congress in Atlanta, Georgia, September.
———. 2001. 'The Implications of Institutional Design for Macroeconomic Performance: Reassessing the Claims of Consensus Democracy'. *Comparative Political Studies* 34 (4): 429–52.
Andeweg, R. B. 2001. 'Lijphart versus Lijphart: The Cons of Consensus Democracy in Homogeneous Societies'. *Acta Politica* 36 (2): 117–28.
Aristotle. 1932. *Politics*. Cambridge and London: Harvard University Press.
Aron, R. 1960a. 'Les institutions politiques de l'Occident dans le monde du XXe siècle'. In *La Démocratie à l'épreuve du XXe siècle*, edited by R. Aron and F. Bondy, 11–42. Paris: Calmann-Lévy.
———. 1960b. *Les grandes doctrines de sociologie historique*. Paris: Centre de documentation universitaire.
———. 1965. *Démocratie et totalitarisme*. Paris: Gallimard.
———. 1981. *Le spectateur engagé. Entretiens avec J.–L. Missika et D. Wolton*. Paris: Julliard.
Bankowicz, M. 1995. *Kulisy totalitaryzmu: Polityczna teoria dyktatury proletariatu*. Kraków: Wydawnictwo PiT.
Bardi, L., and P. Mair. 2008. 'The Parameters of Party Systems'. *Party Politics* 14 (2): 147–66.
Barnes, S. 1968. 'Party Democracy and the Logic of Collective Action'. In *Approaches to the Study of Party Organization*, edited by W. J. Crotty, 103–38. Boston: Allyn and Bacon.
Bellamy, R. 2012. 'Democracy, Compromise and the Representation Paradox'. *Government and Opposition* 47 (3): 441–65.
Benda, J. 1976. *Il tradimento dei chierici*. Torino: Einaudi.
Berger, S. 1979. 'Politics and Antipolitics in Western Europe in the Seventies'. *Daedalus* 108 (1): 27–50.
Beyme von, K. 1985. *Political Parties in Western Democracies*. Aldershot: Gower.

———. 2002. *Parteien im Wandel. Von den Volksparteien zu den professionalisierten Wählerparteien*. Wiesbaden: Westdeutscher Verlag.
Biehl, H. 2005. *Parteimitglieder im Wandel*. Wiesbaden: VS Verlag für Sozialwissenschaften.
Bille, L. 1997. 'Leadership and Party Change: The Case of the Danish Social Democratic Party 1960–1995'. *Party Politics* 3 (3): 379–90.
Birch, A. H. 1964. *Representative and Responsible Government: An Essay on the British Constitution*. London: Allen and Unwin.
Blondel, J. 1997. 'Amateurs into Professionals'. In *Comparative European Politics: The Story of a Profession*, edited by H. Daalder, 115–26. London and Washington: Pinter.
Bobbio, N. 1955. *Politica e cultura*. Torino: Einaudi.
———. 1961. 'Teoria e ricerca politica in Italia'. *Il Politico* 26: 215–32.
———. 1969. *Saggi sulla scienza politica in Italia*. Bari: Laterza.
———. 1984. *Il futuro della democrazia*. Torino: Einaudi.
Bogaards, M. 2000. 'The Uneasy Relationship Between Empirical and Normative Types in Consociational Theory'. *Journal of Theoretical Politics* 12 (4): 395–423.
Boll, F. 2004. 'Entwicklung der Medienbeteiligung politischer Parteien am Beispiel der SPD'. In *Medienbeteiligungen politischer Parteien*, edited by M. Morlok, U. von Alemann and T. Streit, 15–28. Baden-Baden: Nomos.
Brunclík, M., and M. Kubát. 2019. *Semi-Presidentialism, Parliamentarism and Presidents: Presidential Politics in Central Europe*. London and New York: Routledge.
Bull, M. 2015. 'Italian Political Science and Italian Politics: The (Curious) Elephant in the Room'. *Contemporary Italian Politics* 7 (2): 185–201.
Chabod, F. 1961. *L'Italia contemporanea*. Torino: Einaudi.
Collier, D., and J. Gerring, eds. 2009a. *Concepts and Method in Social Science: The Tradition of Giovanni Sartori*. New York and London: Routledge.
———. 2009b. 'Introduction'. In *Concepts and Method in Social Science: The Tradition of Giovanni Sartori*, edited by D. Collier and J. Gerring, 1–10. New York and London: Routledge.
Collier, D., and J. E. Mahon. 1993. 'Conceptual "Stretching" Revisited: Conceptual Innovation in Comparative Research'. *American Political Science Review* 87 (4): 845–55.
Daalder, H. 1983. 'The Italian Party System in Transition: The End of Polarised Pluralism?' *West European Politics* 6 (3): 216–36.
———, ed. 1997. *Comparative European Politics: The Story of a Profession*. London and Washington: Pinter.
Dahl, R. A. 1956. *A Preface to Democratic Theory*. Chicago: University of Chicago Press.
———. 1971. *Polyarchy: Participation and Opposition*. New Haven and London: Yale University Press.
———. 1989. *Democracy and Its Critics*. New Haven and London: Yale University Press.
Doorenspleet, R., and H. Pellikaan. 2013. 'Which Type of Democracy Performs Best?' *Acta Politica* 48 (3): 237–67.
Downs, A. 1957. *An Economic Theory of Democracy*. New York: Harper.
Druckman, J., et al. 2011. *Cambridge Handbook of Experimental Political Science*. Cambridge: Cambridge University Press.
Duverger, M. 1951. *Les partis politiques*. Paris: Colin.
———. 1954. *Political Parties: Their Organisation and Activity in the Modern State*. New York, London, Sydney: Wiley.
———. 1988. *La nostalgie de l'impuissance*. Paris: Albin Michel.
Easton, D. 1953. *The Political System: An Inquiry into the State of Political Science*. New York: Knopf.
Elgie, R. 2011. 'Maurice Duverger: A Law, a Hypothesis and a Paradox'. In *Maestri of Political Science*, Volume 2, edited by D. Campus, G. Pasquino and M. Bull, 75–92. Colchester: ECPR Press.
Esaiasson, P., and S. Holmberg. 1996. *Representation from Above*. Dartmouth: Aldershot.
Farneti, P. 1993. *Il sistema dei partiti in Italia 1946–1979*. Bologna: il Mulino.
Fischer, J., K. Dowding, and P. Dumont. 2012. 'The Duration and Durability of Cabinet Ministers'. *International Political Science Review* 33 (5): 505–19.

Fisichella, D. 2003. *Elezioni e democrazia*. Bologna: il Mulino.
———. 2005. 'Sul filo della memoria'. In *La scienza politica di Giovanni Sartori*, edited by G. Pasquino, 11–21. Bologna: il Mulino.
———. 2014. 'L'importanza delle leggi elettorali'. In *La Repubblica di Sartori, ParadoXa*, edited by G. Pasquino, 8 (1): 77–95.
Floridia, A. 2017. *From Participation to Deliberation. A Critical Genealogy of Deliberative Democracy*. Colchester: ECPR Press.
Friedrich, C. J. 1950. *Constitutional Government and Democracy*. Boston: Ginn.
Galli, G. 1967. *Il bipartitismo imperfetto. Comunisti e democristiani in Italia*. Bologna: il Mulino.
———. 1972. *Il difficile governo*. Bologna: il Mulino.
———. 1975. *Dal bipartitismo imperfetto alla possibile alternativa*. Bologna: il Mulino.
———. 1983. 'Un bipartitismo ancora imperfetto'. *il Mulino* 29 (4): 674–82.
———. 1991. *I partiti politici italiani*. Milano: Rizzoli.
Galli, G., and A. Prandi. 1968. *Patterns of Political Participation in Italy*. New Haven and London: Yale University Press.
Halpern, S. M. 1986. 'The Discorderly Universe of Consociational Democracy'. *West European Politics* 9 (2): 181–97.
Hanning, J. 1984. 'Twenty Years of Polarized Pluralism—Giovanni Sartori'. In *Teoria dei partiti e caso italiano*. Milano: SugarCo Edizioni.
Hoffmann, H., and U. Rosar. 2013. *Ist die Veröffentlichung von Vorwahlumfragen schädlich für kleinere Parteien? Eine Untersuchung anhand eines Online-Experiments zur nordrhein-westfälischen Landtagswahl 2012*. MIP—Mitteilungen des Instituts für Parteienrecht und Parteienforschung, Jg. 19, 83–94.
Horowitz, D. L. 1991. *A Democratic South Africa? Constitutional Engineering in a Divided Society*. Berkeley: University of California Press.
Htun, M., and G. B. Powell Jr., eds. 2013. *Political Science, Electoral Rules, and Democratic Governance*. Washington, DC: American Political Science Association.
Huntington, S. P. 2007. 'Order and Conflict in Global Perspective'. In *Passion, Craft, and Method in Comparative Politics*, edited by G. L. Munck and R. Snyder, 210–33. Baltimore: Johns Hopkins University Press.
Ignazi, P. 2017. 'Sartori's Party System Typology and the Italian Case: The Unanticipated Outcome of a Polarized Pluralism without Anti-System Parties'. *Contemporary Italian Politics* 9 (3): 262–76.
Kaiser, A. 1997. 'Types of Democracy: From Classical to New Institutionalism'. *Journal of Theoretical Politics* 9 (4): 419–44.
Kaiser, A., M. Lehnert, B. Miller and U. Sieberer. 2002. 'The Democratic Quality of Institutional Regimes: A Conceptual Framework'. *Political Studies* 30 (2): 313–31.
Karvonen, L., and S. Kuhnle, eds. 2001. *Party Systems and Voter Alignment Revisited*. London and New York: Routledge.
Katz, R. S., and P. Mair. 1995. 'Changing Models of Party Organization and Party Democracy: The Emergence of the Cartel Party'. *Party Politics* 1 (1): 5–28.
Koole, R. 1996. 'Catch-all or Cartel? A Comment on the Notion of the Cartel Party'. *Party Politics* 2 (4): 507–23.
Kriesi, H. 1998. *Le système politique Suisse*. Paris: Economica.
Kubátová, H., and M. Kubát. 2018. 'Were There "Bystanders" in Topoľčany? On Concept Formation and the "Ladder of Abstraction"'. *Contemporary European History* 27 (4): 562–81.
LaPalombara, J. 1973. 'Political Science and the Engineering of National Development'. In *Political Development in Changing Societies*, edited by M. Palmer and L. Stern, 27–65. Lexington: Heath-Lexington Books.
———. 1986. 'Dipendenze e interdipendenze nello sviluppo della scienza politica italiana'. In *La scienza politica in Italia. Bilancio e prospettive*, edited by L. Graziano, 61–89. Milano: Franco Angeli.
La Stampa. 2009. 'Da unto del Signore a non sono santo: Quando Berlusconi parla di Santità'. *La Stampa* 22 July 2009.

Lakatos, I. 1989. *The Methodology of Scientific Research Programmes: Philosophical Papers. Volume 1*. Cambridge: Cambridge University Press.

Lane, J. E., and S. Ersson. 2000. *The New Institutional Politics: Performance and Outcomes*. London: Routledge.

Lanzalaco, L. 2012. 'Scienza politica e caso italiano: Alla ricerca di una tradizione di ricerca'. *Rivista italiana di scienza politica* 42 (2): 271–94.

Lawson, K., ed. 1994. *How Political Parties Work*. Westport: Greenwood.

Leggewie, C. 2013. 'Nicht rechts, nicht links—aber radikal'. In *Deutsche Kontroversen: Festschrift für Eckhard Jesse*, edited by A. Gallus, T. Schubert and T. Thieme, 127–40. Baden-Baden: Nomos.

Leibholz, G. 1958. *Strukturprobleme der modernen Demokratie (Vorträge und Aufsätze)*. Karlsruhe: Verlag F. C. Müller.

———. 1965. *Politics and Law*. Leyden: A. W. Sijthoff.

Leibholz, G., and H. Reif. 1951. *Verfassungsrechtliche Stellung und innere Ordnung der Parteien*. Tübingen: Mohr Siebeck.

Lenin, V. I. 1961. 'What Is To Be Done?' In *Lenin's Collected Works*, 347–530. Moscow: Foreign Languages Publishing House.

———. 1972. *Państwo a rewolucja*. Warszawa: Książka i Wiedza.

Leoni, B. 1960. 'Un bilancio lamentevole: il sotto-sviluppo della scienza politica in Italia'. *Il Politico* 25: 31–41.

Lijphart, A. 1984. *Democracies: Patterns of Majoritarian and Consensus Government in Twenty-One Countries*. New Haven and London: Yale University Press.

———. 1992. 'Democratization and Constitutional Choices in Czecho-Slovakia, Hungary and Poland, 1989–1991'. *Journal of Theoretical Politics* 4 (2): 207–23.

———. 1994. *Electoral Systems and Party Systems: A Study of Twenty-Seven Democracies, 1945–1990*. Oxford: Oxford University Press.

———. 1999. *Patterns of Democracy: Government Forms and Performance in Thirty-Six Countries*. New Haven and London: Yale University Press.

———. 2001a. *Le democrazie contemporanee*. Bologna: il Mulino.

———. 2001b. 'The Pros and Cons—But Mainly Pros—of Consensus Democracy'. *Acta Politica* 36 (2): 129–39.

———. 2002. 'The Evolution of Consociational Theory and Consociational Practices, 1965–2000'. *Acta Politica* 37 (1–2): 11–22.

———. 2007. 'Political Institutions, Divided Societies, and Consociational Democracy'. In *Passion, Craft, and Method in Comparative Politics*, edited by G. L. Munck and R. Snyder, 234–72. Baltimore: Johns Hopkins University Press.

Linz, J. J. 2007. 'Political Regimes and the Quest for Knowledge'. In *Passion, Craft, and Method in Comparative Politics*, edited by G. L. Munck and R. Snyder, 150–209. Baltimore: Johns Hopkins University Press.

Linz, J., and A. Stepan, eds. 1978. *The Breakdown of Democratic Regimes*. Baltimore: Johns Hopkins University Press.

Lipset, S. M. 1959. 'Some Social Requisites of Democracy: Economic Development and Political Legitimacy'. *American Political Science Review* (53) 1: 69–105.

———. 1960. *Political Man: The Social Bases of Politics*. New York: Doubleday.

———. 1994. 'The Social Requisites of Democracy Revisited: 1993 Presidential Address'. *American Sociological Review* 59 (1): 1–22.

Lipset, S. M., and S. Rokkan, eds. 1967. *Party Systems and Voter Alignments: Cross-National Perspectives*. New York: The Free Press.

Lustic, I. 1997. 'Lijphart, Lakatos and Consociationalism'. *World Politics* 50 (1): 88–117.

Mair, P. 1997. *Party System Change: Approaches and Interpretations*. Oxford: Clarendon Press.

———. 2008. 'The Challenge to Party Government'. *West European Politics* 31 (1–2): 211–34.

———. 2014. 'Concepts and Concept Formation'. In *On Parties, Party Systems and Democracy: Selected Writings of Peter Mair*, edited by I. van Biezen, 71–91. Colchester: ECPR Press.

Marin, B. 1987. 'From Consociationalism to Technocorporatism: The Austrian Case as a Model-Generator?' In *Political Stability and Neo-Corporatism*, edited by I. Scholten, 120–52. London: Sage.
Marx, K. 2011. *Capital, Volume One: A Critique of Political Economy*. Mineola: Dover Publications.
Marx, K., and F. Engels. 2014. *The Communist Manifesto*. London: International Publishers Co.
Massari, O. 1994a. *Come le istituzioni regolano i partiti. Modello Westminster e partito laburista*. Bologna: il Mulino.
———. 1994b. 'Gran Bretagna: un sistema funzionale al governo di partito responsabile'. In *Rappresentare e governare*, edited by O. Massari and G. Pasquino, 25–53. Bologna: il Mulino.
———. 2010. 'Intervista a Giovanni Sartori'. *il Mulino* 2010 (2): 301–25.
———. 2014a. 'Giovanni Sartori and the Italian Second Republic Democracy'. Paper presented at the conference *Giovanni Sartori: 90 Years of a Political Science Legend*, Prague, September 26.
———. 2014b. 'Quando contano i partiti'. In *La Repubblica di Sartori, ParadoXa*, edited by G. Pasquino, 8 (1): 61–76.
———. 2014c. 'Sistemi di partito, effetti dei sistemi elettorali dopo il 1993 e la riforma elettorale'. Paper presented at Istituzioni e sistema politico in Italia: bilancio di un ventennio e prospettive, Perugia, November 2013.
———. 2017. 'Giovanni Sartori and the Institutional Reforms in the Italian "Second Republic"'. *Contemporary Italian Politics* 9 (3): 246–61.
Mastropaolo, A. 1993. 'Dieci anni dopo'. In *Il sistema dei partiti in Italia. 1946–1979*, edited by P. Farneti, 233–73. Bologna: il Mulino.
Merton, R. K. 1965. *On the Shoulders of Giants: A Shandean Postscript*. New York: The Free Press.
Michels, R. 1911. *Zur Soziologie des Parteiwesens in der modernen Demokratie*. Leipzig: Verlag von Dr. Werner Klinghardt.
Morlino, L. 1989. 'Ancora un bilancio lamentevole?' In *Scienza politica*, edited by L. Morlino, 5–52. Torino: Fondazione Agnelli.
———. 2009. 'Legitimacy and Quality of Democracy'. *International Social Science Journal* 60 (196): 211–22.
Morlok, M., and T. Poguntke. 2012. 'Freie Wähler und Kommunale Wählergemeinschaften aus parteienwissenschaftlicher Perspektive'. In *Politik an den Parteien vorbei. Freie Wähler und Kommunale Wählergemeinschaften als Alternative*, edited by M. Morlok, T. Poguntke and J. Walther, 9–23. Baden-Baden: Nomos.
Mosca, G. 1953. *Elementi di scienza politica*. Bari: Laterza.
Mudde, C. 2010. 'The Populist Radical Right: A Pathological Normalcy'. *West European Politics* 33 (6): 1167–86.
Munck, G. L. 2007. 'The Past and Present of Comparative Politics'. In *Passion, Craft, and Method in Comparative Politics*, edited by G. L. Munck and R. Snyder, 32–59. Baltimore: Johns Hopkins University Press.
Munck, G. L., and R. Snyder, eds. 2007. *Passion, Craft, and Method in Comparative Politics*. Baltimore: Johns Hopkins University Press.
Müller-Rommel, F. 2008. 'Demokratiemuster und Leistungsbilanz von Regierungen: Theorie, Methode und Kritik an Arend Lijpharts "Patterns of Democracy"'. *Zeitschrift für Vergleichende Politikwissenschaft* 2 (1): 1–17.
Neumann, S., ed. 1956. *Modern Political Parties. Approaches to Comparative Politics*. Chicago: University of Chicago Press.
Nohlen, D. 2013. *Wahlrecht und Parteiensystem. Zur Theorie der Wahlsysteme*. Opladen: Barbara Budrich.
Nohlen, D., and P. Stöver, eds. 2010. *Elections in Europe: A Data Handbook*. Baden-Baden: Nomos.
Novák M. 1996. 'Démocratie(s) et efficience(s). Y a-t-il un choix constitutionnel supérieur à tous les autres?' *Revue internationale de politique comparée* 3 (3): 689–712.

———. 1997a. 'Is There One Best "Model of Democracy"? Efficiency and Representativeness: "Theoretical Revolution" or Democratic Dilemma?' *Czech Sociological Review* 5 (2): 131–57.

———. 1997b. *Une transition démocratique exemplaire? L'émergence d'un système de partis dans les Pays tchèques*. Prague: CEFRES.

———. 2000. 'Is There an Optimal Model for Democracy?' In *The Challenges on Theories of Democracy*, edited by S. U. Larsen, 370–94. Boulder: Social Sciences Monographs.

———. 2004. 'Les concepts utilisés dans le modèle consensuel de la démocratie: entre Sartori et Lijphart'. In *Penser la politique comparée. Un état de savoirs théoriques et méthodologiques*, edited by C. Thiriot, M. Marty and E. Nadal, 143–59. Paris: Editions Karthala.

Olson, M. 1965. *The Logic of Collective Action*. Cambridge: Harvard University Press.

Ostrogorski, M. 1903. *La démocratie et l'organisation des partis politiques*. Paris: Calman-Lévy.

Panebianco, A., ed. 1989. *L'analisi della politica: Tradizioni di ricerca, modelli e teorie*. Bologna: il Mulino.

———. 2005. 'Teoria politica e metodo comparato'. In *La scienza politica di Giovanni Sartori*, edited by G. Pasquino, 247–65. Bologna: il Mulino.

Pappalardo, A. 2005. 'La competizione in teoria e in pratica'. In *La scienza politica di Giovanni Sartori*, edited by G. Pasquino, 171–211. Bologna: il Mulino.

Pasquino, G. 1982. *Degenerazione dei partiti e riforme istituzionali*. Roma-Bari: Laterza.

———, ed. 2005. *La scienza politica di Giovanni Sartori*. Bologna: il Mulino.

———. 2009. 'Sartori: Democracy, Parties, Institutions'. In *Masters of Political Science*, edited by D. Campus and G. Pasquino, 167–78. Colchester: ECPR Press.

———. 2013a. 'Political Science for What? Giovanni Sartori's Scholarly Answer'. *Rivista italiana di scienza politica* 43 (3): 455–67.

———. 2013b. 'Conclusioni. Bilancio della scienza politica italiana tra professione e vocazione'. In *Quarant'anni di scienza politica in Italia*, edited by G. Pasquino, M. Regalia and M. Valbruzzi, 235–50. Bologna: il Mulino.

———, ed. 2014. 'La Repubblica di Sartori'. *ParadoXa* 8 (1).

———. 2015. 'Italy Has Yet Another Electoral Law'. *Contemporary Italian Politics* 7 (3): 293–300.

———, ed. 2016. *Classico fra i classici: Parties and party systems quarant'anni dopo. Analisi e interpretazione dei mutamenti nei sistemi partitici*. Genova: Erga edizioni.

Pasquino, G., M. Regalia and M. Valbruzzi, eds. 2013. *Quarant'anni di scienza politica in Italia*. Bologna: il Mulino.

Pasquino, G., and M. Valbruzzi, eds. 2012. 'A chiare lettere: l'analisi concettuale nella scienza politica'. *Rivista italiana di scienza politica* 42 (3): 335–429.

Passigli, S. 2001. *Democrazia e conflitto di interessi*. Firenze: Ponte alle Grazie.

———. 2005. 'Un politologo militante'. In *La scienza politica di Giovanni Sartori*, edited by G. Pasquino, 213–46. Bologna: il Mulino.

———, ed. 2015. *La politica come scienza. Scritti in onore di Giovanni Sartori*. Firenze: Passigli Editori.

Pizzorno, A. 1981. *I soggetti del pluralism: classi, partiti, sindicati*. Bologna: il Mulino.

———. 1994. *Le radici della politica assoluta e altri saggi*. Milano: Feltrinelli.

Rae, D. 1967. *The Political Consequences of Electoral Laws*. New Haven and London: Yale University Press.

Rathkolb, O. 2011. 'Neuer politischer Autoritarismus'. *Aus Politik und Zeitgeschichte* 44/45: 56–62.

Regalia, M., and M. Valbruzzi. 2013. 'Introduzione'. In *Quarant'anni di scienza politica in Italia*, edited by G. Pasquino, M. Regalia and M. Valbruzzi, 9–34. Bologna: il Mulino.

Rokkan, S. 1970. *Citizens. Elections. Parties*. Oslo: Universitetsforlaget.

Rose, R. 1992. *What Are the Economic Consequences of PR?* London: Electoral Reform Society.

Sani, G. 2005. 'La polarizzazione rivisitata'. In *La scienza politica di Giovanni Sartori*, edited by G. Pasquino, 153–70. Bologna: il Mulino.

Sani, G., and G. Sartori. 1983. 'Polarization, Fragmentation and Competition in Western Democracies'. In *Western European Party System: Continuity and Change*, edited by H. Daalder and P. Mair, 307–40. Beverly Hills: Sage.

Sartori, G. 1951. *Da Hegel a Marx: La dissoluzione della filosofia hegeliana*. Firenze: Università di Firenze.

———. 1952. 'Scienza politica e conoscenza retrospettiva'. *Studi politici* 1: 52–74.

———. 1953. *Etica e libertà in Kant*. Firenze: Università di Firenze.

———. 1954. 'Lo studio comparato dei regimi e dei sistemi politici'. *Studi politici* 1: 52–74.

———. 1955. *La filosofia pratica di Benedetto Croce*. Firenze: Università di Firenze.

———. 1957. *Democrazia e definizioni*. Bologna: il Mulino.

———. 1959. *Questioni di metodo in scienza politica*. Firenze: Università di Firenze.

———. 1962. 'Constitutionalism: A Preliminary Discussion'. *American Political Science Review* 46 (4): 853–64.

———. 1963. *Il Parlamento Italiano 1946–1963*. Napoli: Edizioni Scientifiche Italiane.

———. 1965. *Democratic Theory*. Detroit: Wayne State University Press.

———. 1966a. 'European Political Parties: The Case of Polarized Pluralism'. In *Political Parties and Political Development*, edited by J. LaPalombara and M. Weiner, 137–76. Princeton: Princeton University Press.

———. 1966b. *Stato e Politica nel pensiero di Benedetto Croce*. Napoli: Morano.

———. 1967. 'La scienza politica'. *Il Politico* 4: 689–701.

———. 1968a. 'Political Development and Political Engineering'. In *Public Policy*, edited by D. Montgomery and A. O. Hirschman, 261–98. Cambridge: Harvard University Press.

———. 1968b. 'Representation: Representational Systems'. In *International Encyclopedia of the Social Sciences*, edited by D. L. Dills, 465–74. New York: Macmillan—The Free Press.

———. 1969. 'From the Sociology of Politics to Political Sociology'. In *Politics and the Social Sciences*, edited by S. M. Lipset, 65–100. New York: Oxford University Press.

———. 1970a. *Antologia di scienza politica*. Bologna: il Mulino.

———. 1970b. 'Concept Misformation in Comparative Politics'. *American Political Science Review* 64 (4): 1033–53.

———. 1970c. 'Per una definizione della scienza politica'. In *Antologia di scienza politica*, edited by G. Sartori, 11–28. Bologna: il Mulino.

———. 1970d. 'The Typology of Party Systems: Proposals for Improvement'. In *Mass Politics: Studies in Political Sociology*, edited by E. Allardt and S. Rokkan, 322–51. New York: The Free Press.

———. 1972. 'La politica come scienza'. *Rivista italiana di scienza politica* 2 (2): 227–63.

———. 1973a. *Correnti, frazioni e fazioni nei partiti politici italiani*. Bologna: il Mulino.

———. 1973b. 'What Is Politics?' *Political Theory* 1 (1): 5–26.

———. 1974a. 'Il caso italiano: salvare il pluralismo e superare la polarizzazione'. *Rivista italiana di scienza politica* 4 (3): 675–87.

———. 1974b. 'Philosophy, Theory and Science of Politics'. *Political Theory* 1 (2): 133–62.

———. 1975. 'The Tower of Babel'. In *Tower of Babel: On the Definition and Analysis of Concepts in the Social Sciences*, edited by G. Sartori, F. W. Riggs and H. Teune, 7–37. Pittsburgh: International Studies Association, Occasional Paper No. 6, University of Pittsburgh.

———. 1976. *Parties and Party Systems: A Framework for Analysis*. New York: Cambridge University Press.

———. 1979. *La politica: logica e metodo in scienze sociali*. Milano: SugarCo.

———. 1982. *Teoria dei partiti e caso italiano*. Milano: SugarCo.

———. 1984a. 'Guidelines for Concept Analysis'. In *Social Science Concepts: A Systematic Analysis*, edited by G. Sartori, 15–85. Beverly Hills, London, New Dehli: Sage.

———. 1984b. 'Pluralismo polarizzato e interpretazioni imperfette'. *il Mulino* 30 (4): 433–34.

———, ed. 1984c. *Social Science Concepts: A Systematic Analysis*. Beverly Hills, London, New Dehli: Sage.

———. 1986. 'Dove va la scienza politica'. In *La scienza politica in Italia. Bilancio e prospettive*, edited by L. Graziano, 98–114. Milano: Franco Angeli.

———. 1987. *The Theory of Democracy Revisited*. Chatham: Chatham House.

———. 1991a. 'Comparing and Miscomparing'. *Journal of Theoretical Politics* 3 (3): 243–57.
———. 1991b. 'Le riforme istituzionali tra buone e cattive'. *Rivista italiana di scienza politica* 21 (3): 375–407.
———. 1991c. 'Rethinking Democracy: Bad Polity and Bad Politics'. *International Social Science Journal* 129 (August): 437–50.
———. 1992. *Seconda Repubblica? Sì, ma bene*. Milano: Rizzoli.
———. 1993. *Democrazia: cosa è*. Milano: Rizzoli.
———. 1994. *Comparative Constitutional Engineering: An Inquiry into Structures, Incentives and Outcomes*. New York: New York University Press.
———. 1995a. *Come sbagliare le riforme*. Bologna: il Mulino.
———. 1995b. *Ingegneria costituzionale comparata*. Bologna: il Mulino.
———. 1996. 'L'Italia tra sbagli e abbagli costituzionali'. Appendix to 1996 edition of *Ingegneria costituzionale comparata*, 221–234. Bologna: il Mulino.
———. 1997a. 'Chance, Luck and Stubbornness'. In *Comparative European Politics: The Story of a Profession*, edited by H. Daalder, 93–100. London and Washington: Pinter.
———. 1997b. *Homo videns: televisione e post-pensiero*. Roma-Bari: Laterza.
———. 1997c. *Studi crociani. I. Croce filosofo pratico e la crisi dell'etica*. Bologna: il Mulino.
———. 1997d. 'Understanding Pluralism'. *Journal of Democracy* 8 (4): 58–69.
———. 1998. 'Il fiasco della bicamerale'. Appendix to 1998 edition of *Ingegneria costituzionale comparata*, 235–41. Bologna: il Mulino.
———. 2000a. 'Incapacità di riforma e bastardi istituzionali'. Appendix to 2000 edition of *Ingegneria costituzionale comparata*, 243–52. Bologna: il Mulino.
———. 2000b. *Pluralismo, multiculturalismo e estranei: saggio sulla società multietnica*. Milano: Rizzoli.
———. 2001. 'Signor Presidente, sul conflitto di interessi non è possibile tacere: lettera aperta'. *MicroMega* (June): 7–12.
———. 2002. 'Conflitto di interessi'. In *Il Governo Berlusconi*, edited by F. Tuccari, 21–33. Roma-Bari: Laterza.
———. 2004a. *Mala tempora*. Roma-Bari: Laterza.
———. 2004b. 'Norberto Bobbio e la scienza politica in Italia'. *Rivista italiana di scienza politica* 34 (1): 7–11.
———. 2004c. 'Verso una costituzione incostituzionale?' Appendix to 2004 edition of *Ingegneria costituzionale comparata*, 219–34. Bologna: il Mulino.
———. 2004d. 'Where Is Political Science Going?' *Political Science and Politics* 37 (4): 785–87.
———. 2005a. *Parties and Party Systems: A Framework for Analysis*. 40th Anniversary Edition. Colchester: ECPR Press.
———. 2005b. 'Party Types, Organisations and Functions'. *West European Politics* 28 (1): 5–32.
———. 2006. *Mala costituzione e altri malanni*. Roma–Bari: Laterza.
———. 2007. 'Il bipolarismo che non funziona'. *Corriere della Sera*, July 20.
———. 2008. *La democrazia in trenta lezioni*. Milano: Mondadori.
———. 2009. *Il sultanato*. Roma–Bari: Laterza.
———. 2012. 'Come fare scienza politica'. *Rivista italiana di scienza politica* 42 (3): 341–54.
———. 2015. *La corsa verso il nulla. Dieci lezioni sulla nostra societa in pericolo*. Roma: Mondadori.
———. 2016. *Elementi di teoria politica*. Bologna: il Mulino.
Schedelen van, M. P. 1984. 'The Views of Arend Lijphart and Collected Criticisms'. *Acta Politica* 19 (1): 19–55.
Schedler, A., and C. Mudde. 2010. 'Data Usage in Quantitative Comparative Politics'. *Political Research Quarterly* 63 (2): 417–33.
Schmitt, H., and S. Holmberg. 1995. 'Parties in Decline?' In *Citizens and the State*, edited by H. D. Klingemann and D. Fuchs, 95–133. Oxford: Oxford University Press.

Schmitter, P. C. 2007. 'Corporatism, Democracy, and Conceptual Traveling'. In *Passion, Craft, and Method in Comparative Politics*, edited by G. L. Munck and R. Snyder, 305–50. Baltimore: Johns Hopkins University Press.

———. 2009. 'The Nature and Future of Comparative Politics'. *European Political Science Review* 1 (1): 33–61.

Schumpeter, J. A. 1942. *Capitalism, Socialism and Democracy*. New York: Harper and Row.

Skach, C., et al. 2009. 'Teacher and Mentor'. In *Concepts and Method in Social Science: The Tradition of Giovanni Sartori*, edited by D. Collier and J. Gerring, 341–46. New York and London: Routledge.

Shugart, M. S. 2008. 'Comparative Electoral Systems Research'. In *The Politics of Electoral Systems*, edited by M. Gallagher and P. Mitchell, 25–56. Oxford: Oxford University Press.

Shugart, M. S., and J. M. Carey. 1992. *Presidents and Assemblies. Constitutional Design and Electoral Dynamics*. Cambridge: Cambridge University Press.

Sola, G. 1989. 'La democrazia rivisitata da Sartori: una nota'. *Rivista italiana di scienza politica* 19 (1): 113–36.

———. 2005. 'La rinascita della scienza politica'. In *La scienza politica di Giovanni Sartori*, edited by G. Pasquino, 23–69. Bologna: il Mulino.

Stepan, A. 2007. 'Democratic Governance and the Craft of Case-Based Research'. In *Passion, Craft, and Method in Comparative Politics*, edited by G. L. Munck and R. Snyder, 392–455. Baltimore: Johns Hopkins University Press.

Strœm, K. 1990. 'A Behavioral Theory of Competitive Political Parties'. *American Journal of Political Science* 34 (4): 565–98.

Truzzi, S. 2014. 'Giovanni Sartori "Il salto con gli sci, Kant per sonnifero e la zuppa in scatola"'. *Il Fatto Quotidiano*, May 5.

Ventura, S. 2016. 'La tipologia dei sistemi di partito e i casi italiani: un analisi logica e empirica'. *Quaderni di Scienza Politica* 23 (3): 387–416.

Vodička, K. 2003. 'Příčiny rozdělení Československa: analýza po 10 letech'. *Politologická revue* 10 (1): 55–64.

Whimster, S. 2003. *The Essential Weber: A Reader*. London: Routledge.

Wiatr, J. J. 1999. *Socjologia polityki*. Warszawa: Wydawnictwo Naukowe Scholar.

Index

Accademia dei Lincei, 57
accountability, 15, 20, 24, 103n10
Allende, Salvador, 22
Almond, Gabriel A., 23–24, 30–31, 52n14
American Association for Political Science, 4
anarchism, 111
Anderson, Liam, 96–97, 102
Andeweg, Rudy B., 99, 101
Andreatta, Beniamino, 13
Andreotti, Giulio, 90n4
Antoni, Carlo, 29
anthropology: Marx's, 107; social, 107
Aristotle, 98, 102, 111
Argentina, 119
Aron, Raymond, 37, 51, 97, 98, 103n9
Astrid Group, 67
Austria/Austrian, 46, 78–79, 103n12
Austrian People's Party, 103n12
'authoritarian oligarchies', 78
authoritarianism, 119; 'bureaucratic', 119
avalutatività, 51n7

Babel, 16
Baden-Württemberg, 80n7
Bankowicz, Marek, 10, 39n3, 105
Barbera, Augusto, 59–60
Barile, Paolo, 60
Barnes, Samuel H., 75
Bassanini, Franco, 60, 67
Bastardellum, 68n2

Bavaria, 78
behaviouralism/behaviouralists, 4, 32, 70, 72–73
Belgium, 71, 99
Berlinguer, Enrico, 55, 90n4
Berlusconi, Silvio, 5, 19, 59–62, 66–68n2
Beyme von, Klaus, 10, 69, 81
Biondi, Pompeo, 28
bipolarism, 20, 60–61, 65–67
Blair, Tony, 78
Bobbio, Norberto, 13, 16, 39n7, 41–43
Bossi, Umberto, 5
Bozzi, Aldo, 56
Brandt, Willy, 78
Brazil, 119
Bull, Martin, 42

Calderoli, Roberto, 19, 68n2–68n7
capitalism, 108, 110
capsizing, 61–62
Carey, John M., 97
Casini, Pier Ferdinando, 58
'cat-dog', viii, 34
Catholic Church, 47
Ceccanti, Luigi, 60
centripetal pluralism, 85
Chabod, Federico, 17
Cheli, Enzo, 60
Chile, 22, 54
China, 34, 39n10

Christian democracy/Christian democratic party: German, 75; Italian, 52n16, 55, 68n2, 83, 85, 90n4
Churchill, Winston, 64
Ciampi, Carlo A., 66
Centro studi di politica comparata, 3, 39n6
cleavages, 73, 83, 88, 98–100
coalition: grand, 58, 93; minimum-sized, 93; multiparty, 96; oversized, 93, 102, 102n3; 'surplus majority', 102n3
Collier, David, vii–viii
Columbia University, 4, 31
communism/communist, 13, 16, 21, 34, 39n4, 73, 79, 83–84, 102n4, 105, 108, 110–113, 114, 115n2, 117
Communist Refoundation Party, 59
comparison, 15, 21, 34, 41, 80n6, 100; case studies, 54, 119; 'small-N', 119
concept: abstract, 43; formation, 7, 8–10, 16–17, 24, 32, 33–35, 38, 43, 50, 51, 52n9, 53, 91, 118–119; high-level, 35; low-level, 35; misformation, 7, 14, 33; of mobilisation, 34; of participation, 34; of pluralism, 35
conceptual analysis, vii–viii, 10, 16
conceptual stretching, 34, 91
connotation, 51n8–52n9
constituencies: single-member, 19–20, 49, 65–66
Constitution/s, 98–99; Czechoslovak, 102n4; European, 52n11; Italian, 54, 56; US, 52n11
constitutional court, 21; Italian, 22, 60, 67
Corriere della Sera, 4, 37, 47, 50, 52n10, 56–58, 68n4
Croce, Benedetto, 2, 7, 11, 28–29, 39n2, 47, 52n13, 105
Czech Republic/Czech, 118–119
Czechoslovakia/Czechoslovak, 93, 101, 102n4, 117

Daalder, Hans, 23, 30
Dahl, Robert A., 1, 15, 23, 35, 100, 118
D'Alema, Massimo, 5, 56–60
D'Annunzio, Gabriele, 47
De Mita, Ciriaco, 56
De Nicola, Enrico, 52n13
decisiveness, 96–98, 101, 103n10

decline: of ideology, 72–73; of parties, 72–73, 75, 79–80n4
'degreeism', viii, 34
'deliberationists', 24
democracy: adjective, 113; alternative, 11, 113; bourgeois, 114; capitalist, 110; centrifugal, 93, 102n2; centripetal, 93, 102n2; communist, 110, 113; competitive, 15; competitive theory of, 6, 23, 28–29, 54; consensual, 64, 91, 95; consensus, 10, 91–103n14; consociational, 93, 102n2; 'continental' type of, 95, 103n6; deliberative, 63; depoliticised, 93; direct, 5, 22, 63, 112–113; economic, 110; illiberal, 35; immediate, 61; elitist, 72; empirical theory of, 6, 101; 'French' type, 103n6; genuine, 113; higher, 113; liberal, 5–6, 11, 45; majoritarian, 5, 54, 60–62, 64, 66, 91–93, 96, 98–100, 102–103n14; mandate, 60–62; mandate theory of, 28–29; national, 113; noncapitalist political, 110; non-consented, 93; 'of coordination', 78; 'of parties', 17; organic, 113; 'other', 113; parliamentary, 62, 64; people's, 39n4; political, 109–110; 'popular', 113; postmodern, 79; 'proletarian', 113; proportional, 61, 64, 66; representative, 64; tout court, 110; unconsolidated, 22; with modifiers, 39n4
Democratic Party (Italian), 20, 56
Democratic Party of the Left, 59
Denmark, 76, 79, 80n6
denotation, 51n8–52n9
determinism, 47, 108, 115
dialectics, 106–108, 115
dictatorship of the proletariat, 106, 111, 114
Dini, Lamberto, 58
direct election of the premier, 62
Dogan, Mattei, 23, 30
Doorenspleet, Renske, 103n15
Downs, Antony, 52n15, 72, 79
Druckman, James, N., 25n3
Duverger, Maurice, 1, 7, 20, 33, 38, 40n20, 45, 69–70, 73, 92, 97, 102n3

Easton, David, 48, 52n14

effectiveness, 10, 95–97, 101–102
efficiency, 10, 95–98, 101, 103n7–103n10
egalitarianism, 112
Egyptian, 113
Eisenstadt, Shmuel, N., 23, 30
electoral system: double-ballot, 95; first-past-the-post, 49, 61–62, 65, 103n11; French-style, 20; Italian 1993—1994, 19; majoritarian, 46, 50, 68n7, 99; mixed, 5, 46; one-round, 50, 65; plurality, 61, 64–65, 103n11; proportional, 6, 20, 26n4, 46, 55, 61, 67–68n7, 95–96, 98, 102–103n12; strong (structured), 46; two-round, 19–21, 42, 49–50, 58–59; weak (nonstructured), 46; with majoritarian effect, 99
empirical vaporisation, 46
Engels, Friedrich, 112
engineering: constitutional/institutional, 7–8, 10, 18, 24, 36, 45–46, 48–49, 53–54, 63, 64, 92, 95–96; electoral, 20, 55, 73
Epstein, Leon, 33
equality: economic, 110; legal, 110; political, 110
Ermetismo, 52n12
Ersson, Svante, 101–102
Eurocommunism, 55
Europe: Central, 117–118; Eastern, 34, 39n4, 73
European Parliament, 78–79
European University Institute in Florence, 4
Evans, Peter B., 119

Fabbrini, Paolo, 60
Farneti, Paolo, 55, 85–86
fascism/fascist, 2–3, 28, 39n5, 41, 47, 52n12
Federation of the Greens, 59
Fini, Gianfranco, 58–59
Finland, 71, 79
Fisichella, Domenico, 20, 40n17, 57, 117
Five Star Movement, 20–22
Florence, 2–4, 13, 28–29, 31
Floridia, Antonio, 24
Folena, Pietro, 59
Forza Italia, 59

France/French, 5, 19–20, 40n20, 52n12, 58, 76, 78, 103n6; Fifth Republic, 19, 40n20, 46, 49, 78, 103n6; Fourth Republic, 22, 54, 103n6; Third Republic, 103n6
Free Democratic Party, 76
Freedom Party of Austria, 79
Frei, Eduardo M., 22
Friedrich, Carl J., 15, 23, 52n14

Galli, Giorgio, 85
Gaulle de, Charles, 78
Gentile, Giovanni, 3, 28
Germany/Germans, 28, 70, 73–76, 78, 80n7, 92, 98; East, 74; Weimar, 21–22, 54
Gerring, John, vii–viii
Goertz, Gary, vii
Gramsci, Antonio, 47
Graziano, Paolo, 55
Great Britain (United Kingdom)/British, 14, 31, 46, 54, 64, 71, 97, 103n12
Green Party, 80n7
Greens, 79
Grillo, Beppe, 61
Guzzetta, Giovanni, 60

Harvard University, 4
Hegel, Georg W. F., 2–3, 7, 11, 15, 28, 105–107, 109, 115n2
Hegelianism, 106
'Heidelberg school', 80n6
'hidden consociationalism', 88
historical materialism, 106, 111
Hungary, 78
Huntington, Samuel P., 1, 40n22
'hypo-citizen', 5

Iceland, 72
ideology: bourgeois, 108; communist, 108; end of, 106; libertarian, 11; majoritarian, 61, 62; Marx's/Marxist, 106, 114, 115; of equality, 11, 113; of freedom, 113; of liberty, 11
Ignazi, Piero, 89
Il Politico, 51n1
'inclusion of preferences', 98
'inclusiveness', 98
India, 34–35, 46

inequality,: economic, 110–111; social, 76
institutionalism/institutionalists, 45, 73
International Political Science Association, 16
Iotti, Nilde (Leonilde), 56
Ireland, 80n6
Israel, 67
Italian Communist Party, 55–56, 71, 85, 88, 89n2–90n4
Italian People's Party, 59
Italian Political Science Association, 26n5
Italian Social Movement, 55, 85, 89n2
Italicum, 22, 68n2
Italy, 3–6, 8–9, 13–14, 16–19, 20–23, 29, 31, 37–38, 41–42, 46–52n10, 54–58, 61–63, 65, 69, 71, 79, 82–85, 117, 119; Fascist, 2, 28; First Republic, 4, 10, 37, 46, 49, 54–56, 60, 61, 65, 83, 88, 118; Second Republic, 4–5, 8–10, 10, 37, 46, 53–54, 56, 60, 66–68, 118

Japan, 34, 80n6

Kaiser, André, 92, 97–98
Kant, Immanuel, 2, 7, 15, 28, 79, 105
Karvonen, Lauri, 18
Katz, Richard S., 73
Kohl, Helmut, 78
Kriesi, Hanspeter, 95
Kubát, Michal, 9, 51n2–52n9
Kuhn, Thomas S., 101
Kuhnle, Stein, 18
Kurtz, Markus, vii

Labour Party, 78
ladder of abstraction, 35, 52n9
Lafontaine, Oskar, 78
Lane, Jan-Erik, 101–102
LaPalombara, Joseph, 43–44
Latin America, 46, 117
Lawson, Kay, 78
Le Pen, Jean-Marie, 76
Lehnert, Matthias, 97–98
Leibholz, Gerhard, 70
Lenin, Vladimir I., 111, 113–114
Leninism, 106
Leonardi, Raffaelle, 55
Leoni, Bruno, 51n6
Letta, Gianni, 59

liberalism, 15, 17, 24, 39n8, 45, 52n11
Lijphart, Arend, 8, 10, 40n14, 64, 73, 91–103n15
Linz, Juan J., 1, 22–23, 30, 32, 119
Lipset, Seymour M., 1, 23, 30, 76, 97

Maccanico, Antonio, 5, 58
Machiavelli, Niccoló, 14, 30, 67
Mair, Peter, 18, 35, 73
majority premium/bonus, 6, 21, 61–62, 66–67, 68n2–68n7
Malaparte, Curzio, 67
Mani pulite, 46
Manzellum, 68n2
Marini, Franco, 59
Marx, Karl, 3, 7, 10–11, 15, 21, 47, 105–115n2
Marxism, 7, 10–11, 28, 105–115
Massari, Oreste, 9, 40n21, 50, 52n10
Mastella, Clemente, 52n16
Mattarella, Sergio, 19, 68n2
Mattarellum, 5–6, 18–20, 46, 49–50, 61, 65–67, 68n6
Matteucci, Nicola, 13
Mejstřík, Martin, 9, 40n18
Merkel, Angela, 78
Merton, Robert K., 15
Metastasio, Pietro, 113
methodology/methods/approach: comparative, 13, 17, 18–20, 22–25, 32–34, 39n12–40n13, 41, 49, 80n6, 91, 118–119; of social sciences, viii, 2, 4, 6–8, 34, 40n14, 48, 51n7, 118; qualitative, vii, 10, 22, 40n13, 71, 118; quantitative, 2, 7, 10, 32–33, 40n13, 48, 52n14–54, 70–71, 74, 77, 79–80n6, 118–119; 'singular comparative', 53; statistical, 32, 40n13, 54, 80n5
Mexico, 34
Michels, Robert, 70
Miglio, Gianfranco, 13
Miller, Bernhard, 97–98
minimal/minimalist definition, 35, 118
Minister for Constitutional Reform, 5, 58
misclassification, 34
Montanelli, Indro, 60
Morlino, Leonardo, 41–42, 103n13, 117
Moro, Aldo, 55, 90n4
Mosca, Gaetano, 29, 39n8, 41

Moscow, 55
Mudde, Cas, 40n13
Müller-Rommel, Ferdinand, 102
multiculturalism, 5, 37
multipolarity, 82–83

Napolitano, Giorgio, 67
National Alliance, 58
National Front, 78
Nazism/national socialism/Nazis/national socialists, 22
neofascist, 17, 71, 83
neoliberalism, 75
Netherlands, 76, 80n6, 95
New York, 4, 27, 31–32, 57, 60
New Zealand, 78, 80n6
Nohlen, Dieter, 80n6
Norway, 34
Novák, Miroslav, 10, 40n19, 68n5
North Rhine-Westphalia, 78
Northern League, 19, 58
'novitism', viii
Nuova Antologia, 25n1

O'Donnell, Guillermo A., 119
Olson, David, 75
one-party state, 34
Orlando, Federico, 60
Ostrogorski, Moisei, 70

Panebianco, Angelo, 59
Panunzio, Sergio, 29, 39n5
ParadoXa, 23
parliament: bicameral/bicameralism, 36; symmetrical (strong), 93; unicameral, 36
parochialism, 34
'participationists', 24
party system: atomized, 46; classification of, 18, 24; extreme multiparty, 22; format of, 7; fragmentation of, 7, 21, 94; 'imperfect bipartism', 85; Italian, 17, 21, 46, 49–50, 54, 56, 71, 79, 82, 83, 85–86, 88; mechanics of, 7, 81; multiparty, 17, 22, 80n6, 102; polarisation of, 7, 89, 94–95; two-party, 17, 64–65, 71; typology of, 7, 10, 69, 71, 81, 84, 87, 94, 118

Pasquino, Gianfranco, 8–9, 14, 31, 37, 42, 46, 55, 57, 59–60, 106, 117
Passigli, Stefano, 37, 44, 55, 57, 60, 67, 117
Pellikaan, Huib, 103n15
Perugia, 29
philosophy, 3, 6, 28–29, 30, 43–44, 105–106, 108–109, 114, 120; classical, 2; Lenin's, 114; Marx's, 109; modern, 3, 29; neopositivist, 43; political, 3, 6, 16, 28, 30, 39n2, 41, 43–44, 47, 105, 108
Phoenix, 113
'Pie Agreement', 59
Pizzorno, Alessandro, 88–89
Plato, 111
pluralism, 35, 88, 103n5; 'centrifugal', 85, 87; 'centripetal', 85; moderate, 71, 94; polarised, 7, 10, 17, 22, 54–55, 71, 75, 81–89n1, 94, 119
Poland/Polish, 39n9, 117
polarisation, 7, 94–95
political correctness, 5
political party: anti-establishment, 84; anti-regime, 85, 87; anti-system, 7, 22, 55–56, 82–85, 89; avant-garde, 113–114; 'bilateral' opposition, 82–83; blackmail, 52n15; blackmail potential/power of, 24, 49, 52n15, 65, 68n6; cartel, 73, 80n4; catch-all, 72, 74, 79; centralized, 78; change, 10, 72, 74–79; coalition potential of, 18, 24; decentralised, 78; delegitimisation of, 86; disillusionment, 72; ecology, 73; environmental, 79; 'étatisation' of, 80n4; extremist, 17, 22, 82; families, 75, 79; fragmentation, 19–20, 49, 65; functions, 69–70; green, 79; hegemonic, 39n9; leadership, 75–78, 87; membership, 73–74, 76, 79–80n4, 88; organization, 10, 69–70, 72, 73–76; 'parliamentary-fit', 54; professionalised, 72, 74–75; 'professional framework', 79; 'professionalised voter', 74–75; 'pro-system', 55, 85; relegitimisation of, 86; relevancy of, 85; sociology of, 10, 73
political science: American, 4, 9, 14, 17, 30–32, 39n12; American-type, 32,

39n12; 'applicable'/applicability of, 3, 8–9, 13–15, 23, 25–26n4, 30, 36, 41–45, 48–51, 118–119; Central European, 117; contemporary, vii, 1–2, 9, 27, 32, 38–40n13, 118–119; empirical, 3, 13, 30, 38, 43–44, 47–48, 51n6; 'illiteracy' in, 40n17, 42; Italian/ in Italy, 3, 9, 13–14, 16, 17, 29–32, 39n6, 41, 47–48, 50–51n5, 57; Weberian style, 51n6
political theory, 2, 6, 8, 10, 27, 53, 105
politics: comparative, 2, 6–8, 10, 14, 27, 33, 38–40n13, 53, 70, 80n6, 91, 105, 118–120n1; 'esoteric', 89; 'invisible', 10, 81–82, 86–90n3; 'visible', 10, 81–82, 86–90n3
'politology', 42
polyarchy, 15, 35
Popper, Karl R., 14, 106
populism/populist/neopopulist, 44, 56, 61, 63, 68, 71, 76; 'direttismo', 63; right-wing, 73, 75–76, 79
Porcellum, 6, 18–20, 22, 67–68n7
postliberalism, 76
premiership: elected, 67; strong, 5, 50, 58, 61, 62, 66; system, 64
presidentialisation, 62
Prezzolini, Giuseppe, 47
Prodi, Romano, 52n16, 58, 66
proportional representation, 20, 26n4, 55, 61, 96, 102, 103n7; 'impure' system of, 95
proporz, 92
Proporzellum, 68n2
Putnam, Robert D., 55

Quasimodo, Salvatore, 52n12
Quirinale Presidential Palace, 66

Rae, Douglas W., 73
rational choice, 70, 77, 79
Rawls, John, 15
reform: constitutional, 4–6, 18–19, 36, 56–58, 60, 66–67; electoral, 19, 46, 50, 55–56, 68n2–68n3, 119; institutional, 18, 51, 60, 62
regime/system: alternating presidential, 36, 38, 49, 58; communist, 102n4; democratic, 5, 8, 25, 36–37, 56, 103n6;

118; liberal democratic, 5; parliamentary, 34, 54, 62, 93; postcommunist, 102n4; semi-presidential, 5, 19, 34, 36, 40n20, 58–59, 62, 103n6
Renzi, Matteo, 22, 56, 68n2
representativeness, 95–98, 101, 103n9
Republican Party, 76
Republic of Salò, 28
revolution, 106, 111, 114; behaviouralist, 32; 'second scientific', 32; theoretical, 101
Rivista Italiana di Scienza Politica, 3, 14, 26n5, 48
Rokkan, Stein, 23, 30, 45, 73, 76
Rose, Richard, 103n7
Rousseau, Jean-Jacques, 11, 113
Russia, 114

Salvi, Cesare, 59
Sani, Giacomo, 40n16, 94, 102
Sartori, Giovanni: applicability of political science, 36, 41–51, 118–119; biography, 2–4, 28–32; career of and work, 2–4, 6–8, 15–17, 23–25; democracy and democratic regimes, 28–29, 91–102; Italian political science, 29–31; Italian politics, 4–6, 17–23, 37–38, 49–50, 53–68; methodology of social sciences/political science, 32–35, 118, 119–120; party politics, 69–80, 81–89; philosophy and political theory, 28–29, 105–115
Scalfaro, Oscar L., 58, 67
Schamis, Hector, 39n11
Scharping, Rudolf, 78
Schedler, Andreas, 40n13
Schmitter, Philippe, 77, 119
Schröder, Gerhard, 78
Schumpeter, Joseph A., 6, 15, 23–24, 28–29, 54, 72
science: 'applied', 42, 44; biological, 40n22; natural, 32; physical, 40n22; social, viii, 1–2, 4, 6–8, 16, 43, 48, 51n7, 57, 118. *See also* political science
Shugart, Matthew S., 97
Sieberer, Ulrich, 97
Slovakia/Slovak, 93
social capital, 119

Social Democratic Party: in Weimar, 22; of Austria, 103n12; of Germany, 74
'societal corporatism', 119
society: heterogeneous/heterogeneity, 94, 102, 103n15; libertarian, 112; 'plural', 93, 95; polarised, 94–95, 102; segmented, 93, 94; 'social and cultural, 95
sociology, 3, 30, 43–44, 47; of parties, 10; of politics, 30, 39n9; political, 30, 39n9
Sola, Giorgio, 13, 31
Spain/Spanish, 40n15, 46, 70, 71, 117, 119; Second Republic, 22, 54
Stalinist, 22
Stanford, California, 4, 31
Stanford University, 4
Stepan, Alfred C., 22, 119
Sting, 31
Strmiska, Maxmilián, 10
Studi politici, 51n1
Stuttgart, 74, 80n7
'sultanate', 68
Sweden, 34
Swiss People's Party, 78
Switzerland/Swiss, 71, 78, 80n6, 98

Tarrow, Sidney, 55
theocracy, 63
'triple alliance', 119
Trump, Donald, 52n11
Turin, 16
Tuscans, 67

'unconstitutional constitution', 63, 67
'ungovernability', 79

Union of Democrats for Europe, 52n16
Union of Soviet Socialist Republics (Soviet Union/Soviet Republic), 34–35, 114
United States of America, vii, 4, 18, 30–32, 52n11
University of Florence, 3, 13
University of Genova, 57
Urbani, Giuliano, 57, 59–60, 117

Valbruzzi, Marco, 25n3
Vassallum, 68n2
Vassallo, Salvatore, 60
Veltroni, Walter, 59, 62
veto/veto power, 92–93; minority, 92–93, 101
Vlaams Blok, 77
Vorwärts, 74
vote: sincere, 21; strategic, 21

Weber, Max, 51n6, 103n14
Westminster, 5, 62, 64–65, 92, 95–96, 101, 102, 102n4
Wiatr, Jerzy J., 39n9

Yale University, 4, 31

Zakaria, Fareed R., 35

About the Contributors

Marek Bankowicz is Professor of Political Science at the Jagiellonian University, Cracow, and one of the leading political scholars in Poland. His research interests include comparative politics and political theory (democratic and nondemocratic regimes, political ideologies). He has published widely in Polish, English and Czech; his most recent books include *Coup d'État: A Critical Theoretical Synthesis* (2012), *Krytycy marksizmu* (2014), *Demokracja według T. G. Masaryka* (2015) and *Maestro politologii: Exploracje polityki Giovanniego Sartoriego* (2018). Bankowicz is also an influential commenter of Polish politics.

Klaus von Beyme is Professor Emeritus of Political Science at the University of Heidelberg and Honorary Professor of Lomonosov State University of Moscow. For his work on parliaments, interest groups, elites, history of political ideas and studies on the relationship of art and politics, von Beyme is rightly considered one of the 'founding fathers' of contemporary political science. Von Beyme is the author of dozens of journal articles, edited volumes and books. He is the recipient of the Schader Award (2008) and the Mattei Dogan Award (2012) by the International Political Science Association for High Achievement in Political Science. He was the president of IPSA from 1982 to 1985.

Giovanni Capoccia is Professor of Comparative Politics at the University of Oxford. His research focuses on democratisation, political extremism, theories of institutional development and European politics. His work has appeared in many international journals and has received several professional awards. He is the author of *Defending Democracy: Responses to Extremism in Interwar Europe* (2005) and co-editor of *The Historical Turn in Democ-*

ratization Studies (2010). He is currently completing a monograph on legal and judicial responses to the extreme right in postwar Western Europe.

Michal Kubát is Professor of Political Science at the Charles University, Prague. In his research and teaching, Kubát focuses on comparative politics (democratic and nondemocratic regimes and politics and government of Central Europe). His work has appeared in Czech, Polish, English and German, and his recent books include *Political Opposition in Theory and Central European Practice* (2010), *Undemokratische Regime: Theoretische Verortung und Fallbeispiele* (2015; with Stanislav Balík) and *Semi-Presidentialism, Parliamentarism and Presidents: Presidential Politics in Central Europe* (2019; with Miloš Brunclík).

Oreste Massari is Professor Emeritus of Political Science and Comparative Politics at the Sapienza University of Rome. His research interests are comparative politics, especially democratic regimes, parties and party systems, electoral systems and Italian politics. He is the author of many journal articles, book chapters and monographs in Italian and English, including *La nuova Politica: Idee, soggetti, istituzioni* (1999) and *I partiti politici nelle democrazie contemporanee* (2004; foreword by Giovanni Sartori). Apart from his scholarly work, Massari is also a publicist and commenter of Italian politics.

Martin Mejstřík is Lecturer at the Charles University, Prague, where he is currently finishing his PhD on Giovanni Sartori and the ability of political science to influence political reality in Italy. Mejstřík completed area studies at the Charles University and political science at the University of Bologna. His research focus includes populism in Europe, South European (in particular Italian) politics and the political theories of Giovanni Sartori. Mejstřík has been the initiator and organiser of the Prague Populism Conferences (held annually since 2015). He was also the co-organiser (with Michal Kubát) of the 2014 conference Giovanni Sartori: 90 Years of a Political Scientist.

Miroslav Novák is Professor of Political Science at the CEVRO Institute (School of Political Studies) in Prague. He is one of the founders of political science as a discipline in the Czech Republic following the fall of communism. After returning from his Swiss exile, Novák joined Charles University in 1990, becoming its first full professor of political science in 2004. His research interests include party systems, theory of democracy and French political science (Raymond Aron, Maurice Duverger). Novák published widely in Czech, French and English, and is—among many other appointments—an editorial board member of the *Czech Sociological Review* and the *Czech Journal of Political Science*.

Gianfranco Pasquino is Professor Emeritus of Political Science at the University of Bologna and senior adjunct Professor of European and Eurasian Studies at The Johns Hopkins University SAIS Europe (Bologna). One of the most widely recognised Italian political scientists, he belongs to the first generation of Sartori's students, later becoming his close collaborator and friend. Besides being a scholar and political commentator, Pasquino was also member of the Italian Senate from 1983 to 1992 and from 1994 to 1996. His most recent books include *La Costituzione in trenta lezioni* (2015), *Cittadini senza scettro* (2015), *Deficit democratici* (2018) and *Bobbio e Sartori. Capire e cambiare la politica* (2019). He has also co-edited the *Oxford Handbook of Italian Politics* (2015).

Maxmilián Strmiska is Professor of Political Science at the Masaryk University, Brno, and University of Hradec Králové, Czech Republic. Strmiska held fellowships at the Universita degli Studi, Pisa, Universita degli Studi, Firenze, Freie Universität, Berlin, Istituto Universitario Orientale, Napoli, University of Manchester and McGill University, Montréal. In his research and teaching, Strmiska focuses on political parties and party systems. Strmiska is the recipient of the Canadian Studies Faculty Enrichment Award Program, the John F. Kennedy Institute for North American Studies Research Grant and the Italian Ministry of Foreign Affairs Scholarship.

www.ingramcontent.com/pod-product-compliance
Lightning Source LLC
Chambersburg PA
CBHW031712230426
43668CB00006B/187